THE TASTE OF LIGHTNING

Ivan V. Lalić (1931–1996) was one of former Yugoslavia's most vital poets. He was also an important translator of poetry; his English translations of his own work appeared in the 1965 inaugural issue of Ted Hughes' and Daniel Weissbort's *Modern Poetry in Translation*. Born and living most of his life in the Serbian capital Belgrade, Lalić is regarded as a grand master of Serbian 20th-century poetry. He went to high school and university in the Croatian capital Zagreb, however. And the Croatian Adriatic – especially around the town of Rovinj, where his family had a house – is a crucial backdrop for many of his poems. Moreover, his poetic world is deeply rooted in Byzantium, the Greek Aegean and Italy. Hence Lalić, perhaps most of all, can be seen as a Mediterranean poet.

Lalić's poems combine a warm sensuality with a love for the natural world, vivid images and similes with thoughtful reflection, here-and-now experience with a backdrop of deep history. In Celia Hawkesworth's words, his work 'crackles with brilliant, arresting imagery forged by the heat of concentrated thought and, above all, it breathes with compassion and humanity'.

Book-length translations of Lalić's work have appeared in six languages, including eight volumes in English: two by his US translator Charles Simic, and six previous editions by his UK translator Francis R. Jones. Lalić's work gained him many prizes at home. His poems in Simic's and Jones's translations have won no fewer than six awards – including the prestigious European Poetry Translation Prize twice.

Ivan V. Lalić

THE TASTE OF LIGHTNING

SELECTED POEMS

EDITED & TRANSLATED BY
FRANCIS R. JONES

Copyright © Estate of Ivan V. Lalić 2025

Translation © Francis R. Jones 1989, 1996, 1997, 2014, 2025

ISBN: 978 1 78037 761 2

First published 2025 by
Bloodaxe Books Ltd,
Eastburn,
South Park,
Hexham,
Northumberland NE46 1BS.

www.bloodaxebooks.com
For further information about Bloodaxe titles
please visit our website and join our mailing list
or write to the above address for a catalogue.

LEGAL NOTICE

All rights reserved. No part of this book may be used or reproduced, stored in a retrieval system, or transmitted in any form, or by any means, electronic, mechanical, photocopying, recording or otherwise, without prior written permission from Bloodaxe Books Ltd.

Requests to publish work from this book
must be sent to Bloodaxe Books Ltd.

The Estate of Ivan V. Lalić has asserted his right – and Francis R. Jones has asserted his right – under Section 77 of the Copyright Designs and Patents Act 1988 to be identified as author and translator respectively of this work.

Cover design: Neil Astley & Pamela Robertson-Pearce.

Printed in Great Britain by Bell & Bain Limited, 303 Burnfield Road, Thornliebank, Glasgow G46 7UQ, Scotland, on acid-free paper sourced from mills with FSC chain of custody certification.

CONTENTS

10 Acknowledgements
11 Introduction

from Time, Fires, Gardens (1961)

21 A rusty needle
23 How Orpheus sang
24 Cathedrals
26 Young love
27 Prayer
28 A voice singing in gardens
30 *from* Four epitaphs
30   *To a dancer*
30   *To a sailor*
30   *To a singer*
31 *from* Orpheus on deck
31   *Song for Eurydice*
33   *Song for the dead*
34 Fresco
36 Byzantium
38 Death with a falcon
39 *from* Melissa
39   *Voices of the dead I*
40   *Morning*
41   *Slavery*
42 The Argonauts
44 Marina
45 Three squalls of rain
47 Love
48 *from* Atlantis
48   *Eye-witness report*
50   *Love: a fragment*

51	Tyrrhenian Sea
52	Inventory of moonlight
54	Roman quartet
54	I
55	II
56	III
57	IV
58	*from* Prolegomena to waking: shores
58	1
58	4

from **Act** (1963)

61	*from* Algol
61	1
62	3
63	4
64	Snowy night
65	Winter letter
66	Winter morning
67	March
68	*from* Spring liturgy for a dead poet
68	1
70	4
72	Young woman from Pompeii
73	Places we love
74	Aosta
75	In praise of the poem
76	Belgrade Airport, June
77	Continent
78	Marina II
79	*from* Nereid
79	3
80	5

from **Circle** (1968)

83	Tomb in Prague
84	Mozart
85	Skopje's monologue
85	1
86	2
87	Waking, one winter night
89	Lyric
90	*from* Love in July / 2
91	Orange
92	Photographs: a romance
94	Joanna from Ravenna
94	1
95	2
96	*from* Dubrovnik, a winter's tale
96	*The masons*
97	*Portal: pietà*
98	*The Dark Province*

from **Of the Works of Love, or Byzantium** (1969)

101	Of the works of love
102	Memory of an orchard
103	* * *
104	The sea described from memory
105	Song of the statue in the earth
106	Byzantium VII

from **Fading Contact** (1975)

109	Winter sea
110	Marina V
111	Genius loci
112	Fiesole, rain

113   Belgrade from old photographs
113   1
115   2
116   3
117   Cantico delle creature
118   Letter to John Berryman
120   *from* Athos in five songs
120   *Daphne*
121   *On the way to Esphigmenou*
122   *Byzantium VIII, or Chilandari*
124   Mnemosyne
124   1
125   2
126   3
127   4
128   To sons growing up

from **The Passionate Measure** (1984)

131   A note on poetics
132   The spaces of hope
133   The raven's monologue
134   Elegy, or the Danube at Donji Milanovac
136   Five letters
136   1
137   2
138   3
139   4
140   5
141   Étude
142   Looking glass
143   Morning Argolid
144   Acqua alta
144   1
145   2
146   3

from **Script** (1992)

149   In praise of sleeplessness
151   Octaves on summer
153   *from* Strambotti
153   1
153   2
153   3
154   4
154   5
154   8
155   9
155   10
156   Never lonelier
157   Pietà
158   Sea

from **Four Canons** (1996)

162   *from* First canon
162   3
163   4
164   *from* Second canon
164   2
165   5

176   TRANSLATOR'S NOTES
176   ABOUT THE TRANSLATOR

ACKNOWLEDGEMENTS

I am grateful to Ivan V. Lalić, who first believed in my translations, and who is a much-missed friend. Thanks too to Svetlana Šeatović Dimitrijević, the late Aleksandar Jovanović, and the late Vladimir Kašnar for their textual advice and support. Finally, I am very grateful to Branka Lalić for her constant encouragement over the years.

Earlier versions of poems selected here appeared in:
    Ivan V. Lalić, *The Passionate Measure* (London, Anvil Press Poetry/ Dublin, Dedalus Press, 1989);
    Ivan V. Lalić, *A Rusty Needle* (London, Anvil Press Poetry, 1996);
    Ivan V. Lalić, *Fading Contact* (London, Anvil Press Poetry, 1997);
    Ivan V. Lalić, *Walking Towards the Sea / Koraci prema moru* (Belgrade, Univerzitetska biblioteka „Svetozar Marković", ed. Aleksandar Jovanović & Svetlana Šeatović Dimitrijević, 2014);
    Comparative Critical Studies (Issue 11/1, 2014);
    Modern Poetry in Translation (Issue 3, 2017).

INTRODUCTION

Ivan V. Lalić was one of late 20th-century Yugoslavia's most talented poets. His poetry has been translated into over 20 languages, and has won many awards, including six prizes in the UK and USA. This book presents a new selection of Lalić's poems in English translation. Some are appearing in English for the first time. Others are revised versions of work published previously, in books now out of print.

A life in poetry
Ivan V. Lalić was born in Belgrade, the Yugoslav and Serbian capital, in 1931. He spent his childhood summers on the slopes of Mount Maljen in western Serbia. This idyll ended brutally – when the Nazis invaded Yugoslavia in 1941, and then with the Allied bombing raids on Belgrade in 1944, in which several of his friends died. As Lalić explained in a BBC interview, 'my childhood and boyhood in the war marked everything I ever wrote as a poem'. 'A Rusty Needle', the opening poem of his first collection, *Once a Boy (Bivši dečak)* of 1955, describes this legacy, and his poetic mission: to 'grow on', with his dead friends' 'gaze in the nape of my neck, like / A rusty needle just under the skin; but also, slowly, / To come to love the night and her soft stars again'.

In 1946, Lalić moved with his parents to Zagreb, the capital of Croatia – like Serbia, a constituent *republika* of the new Socialist Federal Republic of Yugoslavia. There, at the age of 15, a second tragedy struck – but also the beginning of a lifelong happiness: 'the early death of my mother, compensated for by the crazy luck of meeting a girl [Branka] who was to return my love and become my wife and muse in the same person', as he wrote to me decades later.

Ivan V. Lalić studied law, followed by comparative literature, at Zagreb University. He then worked for Radio Zagreb as a literary editor. In 1961, with several poetry collections to his name, he was invited to become Secretary of the Yugoslav Writers' Union. Hence Ivan, Branka and their baby son Vlajko (the first of two boys) moved to Belgrade. Here he spent the rest of his working life, as an editor at two publishing houses, interspersed by a second term as Secretary of the Writers' Union. Besides producing 14 books of poetry, he wrote a radio drama, and was active as a critic and anthologist. He also translated anthologies of French, German, and (with Branka) American and UK poetry.

The family had a house in the historic Croatian coastal town of Rovinj, on the Istrian peninsula. Alongside Belgrade, this was Lalić's other and no less seminal poetic home: the landscapes and seascapes of the Adriatic imbue many of his poems.

It was also the site of a third tragedy. In 1989, Vlajko was skippering a yacht from Rovinj to Venice. A storm blew up, and the boat began to sink. It had just two lifejackets: as skipper, Vlajko gave them to his two crew. They survived, but he did not. This loss is not mentioned explicitly in Lalić's work. But it is the sub-text of two poems written soon afterwards – 'Pietà' (the mother is also Branka, in the Venice morgue), and 'Sea': 'Whatever you might plunge into the sea / Is lighter by the weight of pain displaced'.

During the early 1990s, mutually exclusive nationalisms, violence and war brought about Yugoslavia's disintegration; the conflict also meant that Lalić, as a Serb, could no longer visit Rovinj. As with Vlajko's death, this is not directly referred to in his work. His last poetry collection, *Four Canons (Četiri kanona)*, however, arguably bears the imprint of both losses, of son and country: in it, he questions whether the world runs to a divine plan, and what this plan might be. Lalić passed away suddenly, in 1996, soon after *Four Canons* was published.

'A thicket of song': Lalić's poetic work

Lalić's poetry – vivid and sensual, but also deeply thoughtful – has gained widespread admiration. Bernard O'Donoghue, for instance, praises Lalić's 'irresistible blend of private lyricism and public force'.

And for Judy Gahagan, his poetic voice is 'vital and intense', with a 'magisterial transcendent quality'.

Lalić's earlier poems, which he curated into the definitive selection *Time, Fires, Gardens (Vreme, vatre, vrtovi)* of 1961, tend to be accessible and figurative. Many, however, are already anchored in a wider European and Mediterranean heritage: Orpheus and Marina, Atlantis and Byzantium. Some use free verse. Others use traditional forms – most frequently the classic hendecasyllable (11-syllable line), often rhymed, as in 'How Orpheus sang':

> A thicket of song, with every note a rose;
> A voice of copper, of fruit and foam; a space
> Where every branch outstretches, lengthens and grows
> Softer beneath the bark, as if to expose
> Its blackened body to a woman's embrace.

During the late 1950s and early 1960s, Lalić's imagery grows richer and more expansive – sometimes with echoes of mid-century surrealism, as in the Melissa cycle. In his 'middle period' of the 1960s and 1970s, his imagery becomes more grounded again, though no less sensual than before. But Lalić's startlingly apt use of simile, a hallmark of his earlier work, continues – as in 'Lyric': 'At dawn, frost is on the peach blossom / Like salt on a wound'. Moreover, most of his middle-period poems are in free verse:

> Solstice in the high hills, clear fires
> Printed on the young skin of summer, vultures
> Hatching in roses of air, cataracts
> Of smoky silver oxidising on the slopes
> Between the flowers and bright tatters of wind on the pines
>
>   ['Aosta']

His poems of this period often have a more meditative, thoughtful tone. This comes especially to the fore in his later work, of the 1980s and 1990s. Lalić's last two collections, *Script (Pismo)* of 1990 and *Four Canons* of 1996, also experiment with poetic form.

All the poems in *Script* use fixed metres, and many use rhyme:

> We are twin foci of the same ellipse,
> The orbit of a body that's unknown –
> A star? Or light which thinks of weight, perhaps,
> Along its journey's gyre out there alone?
>
>   ['Strambotti 9']

And *Four Canons* takes its shape from the Orthodox 'canon': a hymn formed of nine odes on nine songs from the Bible, each ending with an address to the Virgin.

Identities and themes

Ivan V. Lalić was a poet of multiple identities. Firstly, a Serbian poet. He saw himself as an heir to the early-20th-century Serbian symbolists like Milan Rakić (quoted in 'Belgrade from Old Photographs'), and Serbian critics rightly view him as a towering figure in their country's poetry. Some of his poems are set in and around his Belgrade home. Others ('Death with a falcon', say) engage with Serbian history, or the wider heritage of Orthodox Christianity (such as the cycle telling of his journey to Athos, the faith's heartland). All these threads lead back to Byzantium, the theme of several poems and cycles: the medieval Serbian state grew up in the Byzantine Empire's shadow, and did not long outlast its fall. And ultimately back to ancient Greece, which also features in several poems (e.g. 'The Argonauts').

The upsurge of us-versus-them nationalisms in Yugoslavia, which caused the country's traumatic break-up, had its counterpart in culture: 'our' literature – Serbian or Croatian, say – has nothing in common with 'theirs'. This has made it unfashionable to see Lalić as having a second, Yugoslav poetic identity, rooted in Yugoslavia's multiple cultures. Yet Lalić's archetypally Yugoslav amalgam of Serbian and Croatian experience was crucial not only in his life path, but also in his poetry. Thus many of Lalić's poems look not only south-east, to Byzantium, but also west, to the Croatian

Adriatic (Rovinj, Dubrovnik). And further, to Italy (as in 'Aosta' or 'Acqua alta'), a key inspiration for Croatian Adriatic culture.

A third identity is simply that of European poet. Lalić wrote in the European modernist mainstream of Yeats and Eliot, of Hölderlin, Rilke and Valéry – poets whom he sometimes alludes to or quotes in his work.

But fourthly, and crucially, I recall Lalić telling me that he saw himself as a Mediterranean poet. I cannot swear to this: memories erode and become re-edited over time. But it feels apt. This identity links his south-eastern and western heritages, just as the Aegean and Adriatic are adjacent arms of the Mediterranean Sea. And in voice and theme, Lalić has an affinity with other 20th-century Mediterranean poets, like Seferis, or Montale (the subject of 'Elegy, or the Danube at Donji Milanovac').

This Mediterranean identity is borne out by Lalić's word use. Of all the content words in the poems collected here (that is, excluding words like 'the', 'of', or 'as'), the most common, at 106 occurrences, is 'sea' (plus 'seas', 'sea-spray', etc.). The sea, in fact, is the subject or background for many of his poems.

More widely, Lalić's poetic world is natural, bright with the freshness of experience – a world of wind and night, of water and air (his third, fourth, fifth and ninth most-used words respectively). This also makes him a wonderful poet of love (at 93 mentions, his second-favourite content word in this collection):

Quiet, phosphor mornings of love,

As the room blossoms into a hall of mirrors
Duplicating a single movement, or maybe the colour
Of a dress on a chair

['Roman quartet II']

But Lalić is more than merely a nature and love poet. His seventh most common keyword is 'word' itself, used no fewer than 57 times. His poems often probe the relationship between the world and the words we use to speak or write about it. Retelling, for instance, fixes the freshness of experience in memory (another keyword in Lalić's poetry), but also distances us from it:

> Images I barter for the right to pronounce them,
> Names I slip as a bribe to time,
> And birds I ring with the thin silver of memory
>
> ['Algol 4']

More widely, many of Lalić's poems are based in personal experience, but suddenly open into another, wider dimension – as when 'each interval of trepidation' between the flashes of a lighthouse is 'enough for a birth or a death' ('Marina V'). Similarly, Lalić's history- or myth-based poems do not merely chronicle. They explore the nature of personal and cultural memory, of what gets through and what is lost forever:

> Is there a choice, is there an order
> In the long migration of landscape into landscape, wall
> Into emptiness, emptiness into tree, into shadow,
> Shadow into hope, hope into wall?
>
> ['Mnemosyne 3']

Translating Ivan V. Lalić

I first met and came to love Lalić's poetry as an undergraduate language student in 1970s Britain. On a postgraduate study year in Sarajevo a couple of years later, I sent him a letter telling of my enthusiasm for his poetry, and enclosing some translations. To my surprise, he not only warmly replied, but a few weeks later we were meeting in Belgrade to plan an English-language selection of his work. Lalić, as a poetry translator himself, was the translator's perfect source poet: friendly and encouraging, thorough in spotting errors and adding key background information, but never insisting on an English solution.

In his home country, Lalić was a renowned master of poetic form.

His shifts between formal and free verse, for instance, were key waypoints on his poetic path, and I have tried to show this through similar shifts in English. But I have also striven to recreate his use of alliteration and sound harmony. Plus, more widely, the warmth of his tone, style and voice, as it moves between vivid and pensive, simple and complex – sometimes in the same poem.

Translating poetry is rarely straightforward, of course. But if one combines painstaking thesaurus and dictionary searches with judicious dashes of creativity, and many rounds of revision, it is nearly always possible to shape an English-language poem that reflects the original's content and style. Sometimes, as in 'How Orpheus sang' above, I reproduced Lalić's original syllabic metres. More often, however, I replaced them with English cultural equivalents, like iambic pentameters.

When rhyme enters the picture, it is famously impossible to find a target-language rhyme scheme that faithfully recreates the source poem's wording. Then I tried instead to stay true to the intent and imagery of Lalić's line, while following the grain of the English wood I was working. In 'Orange', for example, the 7-line original (plus a literal English translation) begins and ends:

Zemlja i vatra i vazduh i voda [The] earth and [the] fire and [the] air and [the] water
U mesu ovog savršenog ploda In the flesh of this perfect fruit
Traju za taj trenutak: biti zreo. Last for that moment: being ripe.
[…] […]
Biti ceo. Being whole.

My final version converts Lalić's hendecasyllables into iambic pentameters, but keeps his AAB[…]B rhyme scheme:

The water and the earth, the fire and air
Inside this perfect fruit last till they bear
Flesh: the moment of ripeness that's their goal.
[…]
Being whole.

I felt that the first and last lines were crucial to the poem's narrative arc, so I kept them as literal as possible. This meant recasting the wording of lines 1–2, over hours of searching, brainstorming and redrafting, to keep the original rhyme scheme while trying to convey the key elements of Lalić's image. My only regret is that the final version has lost the 'biti ceo / biti zreo' ('being ripe / being whole') echo, but you can rarely win 'em all as a poetry translator.

'Song' and 'poem' are the same word in Serbian: 'pesma'. Lalić's poetry does not *speak* to the heart and mind, it sings to them. Inevitably, my English translations sing a slightly different tune than his originals. But I hope that they manage to convey Ivan V. Lalić's talents as a grand master of European poetry.

FRANCIS R. JONES

FROM
Time, Fires, Gardens

Vreme, vatre, vrtovi

1961

A rusty needle

Then I came to love the night, to love it for the wind
Teased through the dark needles of the pines,
And the shutter rapping at the window of the solid house,
Whose foundations and the green rust of weeds are all that remain.

When there was no wind, the crickets stayed,
And my mother's breath, rightwards in the dark,
Lukewarm and gentle. I sank into sleep as if into soapy water,
Quickly, softly, leaving no ripple on the surface.

Summers on the mountain's shoulder, between the cones;
In the wind, beneath my dark skin, my small bones
Grew. Guests would arrive at the green-eyed house,
While I was grubby with resin from the pines.

Autumn – that was the city. The gentle fall of a street
Spanned with the triumphal arch of children's laughter.
Little expeditions in the shadow of a big world
Beginning to shake on its feet of clay.

Oh, there were so many of us. Each a meek cadet
Of a green life that loved us all alike. Citizens soon
And castaways, still all in the cocoon,
Sissies and rowdies, squid-soft still.

Yet we were caught in a net, like a salty sea-crop
Shimmering, viscid, through the chilly depths.
I lived to see a summer in a wounded city,
My mouth full of fear like ground glass.

Then I came to hate the night, to hate it for the fear
Teased through the echo of footsteps in the street.
For a full-grown childhood plucked to the blood,
Feathers flying on a blade of black breath.

I think of those who were born alongside me,
Those now lying deep in their deaths. Each
A meek cadet of a green life, who outgrew me
By a death, all of a sudden, against their will.

Did they really come of age in an instant,
Before they crumpled like poppies under the scree
Of rubble, their eyes full of fear and dust, dumbstruck
Because this was not what they wanted to be?

I don't know. But I remained, to grow on
With their gaze in the nape of my neck, like
A rusty needle just under the skin; but also, slowly,
To come to love the night and her soft stars again.

The woods remained too, and the big wind
Teased through the needles of the felled pines,
Red-grey cities which I will enter, a sprig
Of familiar weeds crushed in my wet fist.

And, between two vertebrae, a sliver of fear:
The remnant of a death which passed quite near.
And rickety bridges into bubbles of distance
Which I walk, fairly resolutely, in thinned file.

How Orpheus sang

A thicket of song, with every note a rose;
A voice of copper, of fruit and foam; a space
Where every branch outstretches, lengthens and grows
Softer beneath the bark, as if to expose
Its blackened body to a woman's embrace.

The beasts of the field and forest scarcely sensed
The moment their blood congealed to mead. Yet here
They stand, the large with the small, all bristling, tensed;
Sculpted, it seems, where the silence has condensed,
A lake of light in every attentive ear.

In his singing, time is translated to sound,
Softened into the limpid, protean form
Of shallow water where red-dappled trout abound,
The speckled tints of flowered and grassy ground,
And the taste of sunlit soil, humid and warm.

And he sings his song in the gentle, pouring rain,
In the purple clover; the raw flesh pulsates
Under his skin; but his ears secretly strain
For a wiser voice to echo the refrain
Beneath the stone, where silence's first wave waits.

Cathedrals

And earth felt stone no longer wanting
To be stone, as heavy as the sea is blue.
Grown lighter for the sake of darkness, of love
For a bird-filled heaven lying just above the woods,
Stone foamed into the lace of buildings, storming
Space and seizing it from the bewildered birds.
This is how miracles came about – bright, uncertain,
Still wet with pure blue swirls of wind.

But the stone stayed stone.
As the blunted chisels know, and the birds.

It was naïve, with hindsight, to invite
A triple god to take up lodging in these tenements
With their flimsy, ornately shored-up walls:
Since when did gods live in affordable miracles?
But this stone miracle became overgrown
With a world, with leaves, with unyielding forms
Which the winds have long since learned by rote,
Wearing their fingers to the bone. And the sun is forced
To smile each time it wants to pass through multicoloured glass
Into a space where every sound is peeled back to the core.

Stone soared in the wind, like a wave of foam.
But the stone stayed stone.

You'll have to ask the dead masons if they believed
In stone blossoming weightless in the sun
Like a chestnut tree, and growing into
The yielding sky, and that none of this would end;
Or if they knew that, in an instant,

Mid-way, stone would dimly wish
To be stone again, as heavy as sea is blue.
Because miracles happened, bright and uncertain,
As incomplete as spring, as a tree.

With a bird-filled heaven close enough to touch.

Young love

She'll fall asleep, a shoal of goldfish between
Her lashes now combing the dark. She'll fall asleep,
A touch of tiredness deep in her rounded joints:
Sleep, her tiny earwig, waits on her pillow.

She'll fall asleep to the creak of dark furniture,
Beneath the shadows of leaves that flit across
The pane, her hands left slightly at a loss
By all she has touched, open and still half-awake.

She'll spin a spider's web of breath about her;
And a cat, more quietly than itself, will cross
The room. A sharp moon will run its inquisitive
Birchtwig fingers across her already-warm bed.

She'll fall asleep. The tick of the clock, like a mouse,
Is nibbling the silence. She'll dream she's up and running
On tiptoe down the wind-blue street, chasing
The day which long since slipped away from the house.

Prayer

Upon this earth, o love, thy will be done
As in this heaven, dreadfully unsure.
The season of the colours has begun,
The south wind's breaking into leaf once more;

Like shallow wells, the light-blue nights are filled
With stars, and feel as soft as ripe fruits' skins.
Let people love each other as they will,
In temporary circles of small things.

Here in these towns, o love, thy will be done,
Down all the streets whose wanderlust is spent,
And who will never break their ranks and run;

Where leaves, unwounded still, spread out their shawls,
Between these folk who call themselves content
Because they trust their ancient harbour walls.

A voice singing in gardens

How can I hunt down the voice that's swimming out of me
Like a bird from the sky, and becoming a stranger,
Self-sufficient and conscious of its own existence,
The voice that innocently mocks its homeland
Of blood and gentle ignorance, as it sings somewhere
In its own pure sphere, which my wounded fingers
Cannot fumble after, and whose boundaries
My long-cheated gaze cannot grasp? (Perhaps at the top
Of the stair?) How can I hunt down the voice
Born once in the flesh of my first awakening
Like a weird, blind stranger, maturing more quickly,
The voice now singing in the green space of gardens
On the far side of hearing, now transformed into a bird?

Timidly, afraid of breaking some law
I do not know, I sneak past the walls,
The latticed walls of waking, with the first signs
Of a numb fatigue in the movements of my limbs.
To whom can I confess this futile hunt,
Who can I ask, in the plain of sun and blue tar,
On the bench beneath the avenue of petrified trees,
Who can I ask about the voice in the gardens?
People lean their arms on their usual tables,
Dip bread into salt, laugh or go away,
Usually through the door, and disappear into themselves,
Or without themselves. As for the dead, who I'm afraid
To ask in case they know far, far too much,
They do not notice us as they concentrate on
Carefully dismantling their former fates,
Like watchmakers – they're outside the gardens, anyway.

And yet, perhaps, a tree is left in the wind,
A street, and a brief ripening of duration,
A few broken toys, and the voice is left,
A voice which once lived here
But now sings in gardens.

from **Four epitaphs**

To a dancer

The secret of your going is locked into the moment
You groped, like someone suspicious and blind,
For the back of the known. A movement which blossomed
Into the rose-coloured foam of a childhood orchard.
A movement in which you peeled off the shadow
Heavier than you, since it was truer to earth.
And now, those who love you can dream of a fiery
Black rose beneath a hill of blue, transparent ice.

To a sailor

In the end, the sea smoothed away its wrinkles.
He is left cradled in the warm lap of the current.
His arms outflung, he listens hard; turning
On a rose of drowned winds, he dips
Like a blunted compass needle, seeking
A course for a shore.

To a singer

Here lies the sworn interpreter of a green
Tongue. Dust has populated his deserted lips.
Has anyone ever looked death in the ear
As if in an iron well, an echoing well,
To see their voice turn to stone and drop to shatter
The silence at the bottom, but the bottom does not exist?

from **Orpheus on deck**

Song for Eurydice

No one stopped me plunging my voice,
Plated in violet silver, into your darkness,
Your thick darkness devoid of time;
But my voice melted on your sweaty palms, choked
On black feathers from layers of dead birds,
Vaporised on the coals of wisdom in your eyes,
And now, gnawed to the bone by the walls' invisible sneers,
I return alone.

Lords of the far side of duration, were it not
For the love that suffused my crimson fear, as the
South wind is wet with the scent of the sea,
I would not have knocked at the doors of that forbidden return.
But you let me tell the sands of dead time, and
Spattered me with your knowing, silent laughter
When I believed my blood-heavy eyes.

I was alone, you see. And I walked
Your passageways, only to stay so.
But still I robbed your darkness of a little light
And touched your tranquil lips and limbs,
To understand the senseless meaning of my loss.
Eurydice, unravelled like a tree into its roots,
Lasts on outside me, without a farewell wave.

And now, gnawed to the bone by the walls' invisible sneers,
I dig my nails into my dumbstruck, ashy palms,
To leave as I came, with dignity, to keep myself

From crying out, from running for the doors of the sun,

Afraid, and hideously enriched.

Song for the dead

Nobody dies too late, O lords of the far side
Of curiosity, nobody ever dies too late
To find an open door. Someone will be waiting to wipe
The blood in silence from their frightened lips, to name
Them once and for all. This much I know – I who, by
A game of miracles, can breathe deeply again, beneath
A sky furrowed like a shell by the knives of wind, though
I wished to break the bread of death with clean fingers.

There's still a lot left on this side of curiosity:
The tarnished silver dripping from your mirrors,
The marrow of wisdom sucked with toothless gums
From the broken bones of time, a barren light
Grown old in the eyes of amber, corridors
Of resinous tears, red walls of silence which open
Only to a knocking from within, the naked
Roots of what was once a dream, fruitlessly watered
From the outside by the tears of the unknowing,
Oh all I clumsily called your sort of happiness,
Confused by your tranquillity, confused by your roses
Which fleshily unfold under an inner moonlight.

Afraid, I underestimated you, o lords of the
Back of this duration. Forgive me my mistake.
For who could have known the price of the power I gained
To stay silent about it all? Who could have known
The secret rule of our common game: that no one can win,
Because the stakes must stay unchanged? Oh, now I know
That you listen to the motion of the same sea,
Only with sharper ears. You fear the same gods.

But now I no longer know your sort of happiness,
And so I respect you, unknown lords
Of my love who stayed behind in the long tunnel,
Weightless and blue as a will-o'-the-wisp,
Named once and for all, outside me.

Fresco

Angry angel on the verge of pure flame,
The contorted air ignites at your gaze, which recalls
The forgotten: you emerge from the wall, armed
And solemn, as you once emerged from a night
When it was complete, despising the illusory
Pattern of stars, for you were now white-hot
With the perilous beauty that inseminates time.
Angry angel on the verge of pure flame,
If you step forth, the wall will surely crumble,
But your splendid miracle will stay.

Forgive me my weakness.

Angry angel with your smile of invisible light,
The night is now tame behind your shoulder
Which bears an arm untired by its gesture
Of warning. But who will stay buried beneath
This solid wall, if you should step forth?
Filled with yourself, you do not explain your existence,
Just like the wind, which hides in fear of you
Inside the little eye of the candle. Angry angel,
I have come from a space beyond these walls to find
The golden honeycomb between the jaws of your silence.

Forgive me my mortality.

Angry angel on the verge of pure flame,
The night is large from which you emerged,
I fear I'll disappear before you notice me.

Lead me not into fear.

Byzantium

Image on a golden ground, innocent blush
Of an ageing sun, I sing you this because I love you,
Dead miracle, detested beauty whose marble bones
Lie buried beneath the grass and cypress trees;
I think of you with pride, hoarding a little
Of your wise gold deep in my eyes, which sprouted
Like flowers out of the earth, having slowly absorbed
Your last few drops of blood, cruel mistress.
I hate the hatred that dawns like the premature child
Of impotent spite in the disbelieving eyes
Which drift from the forests of the setting sun.
Oh, how they despised you, miraculous dead light!

> *Here the domes of palaces*
> *Rose like golden chalices,*
> *Whilst in the lands to the west*
> *Everything simply regressed:*
> *Gangs of malodorous knights*
> *Whose pastime was hunting lice.*

Beauty is never forgiven, nor is a lonely wisdom,
Torn frontier with two wide worlds flowing
Through your blood. Look, you were still heavy
With marble gods who had fallen asleep, eyes open, beneath
The thin grass. For the blue-lipped shores were the same,
After all, under the same sun. The same olives.
But all was softer now, with an ominous ripeness.
The ripeness of the agave. Like the gazes of the emperors
On the steps. Perhaps with a touch of ennui.
Too many images, noble and cruel, drowned in the pools
Of beautiful women's eyes. And the walls have started to sing.
But the borders are retreating like an obedient sea.

A rabble of western knaves
Come stumbling out of their caves.
At writing Charlemagne's quick,
He knows some arithmetic.
Grown older, our sun sinks low,
A bubble the breezes blow.

Twofold wisdom, grove of silver cypress trees
Misty with incense – cruel mistress,
You befuddled, rank by rank, even the visored eyes
Of barbarians with crosses on their famished bellies.
They raped you, then you ate them, horses and all.
You, dead light, were the first to hear the distant drumming
Of a grim and dusty green cavalry on the flank
Of your world. All that remains in the end is a city
On a neck of sea, encircled by the crimson eyes of fire,
And gazes teeming feverishly in her towers
And cast into the callous void of a sea
Without sails. They forgot you, beauty of the world,
Because they wanted to. Your blood be on their heads.

We're not uncaring, far from it –
But face those guns of Mahomet?
We'll send the politest of tears
To comfort those Greek buccaneers.
And why doesn't Constantine call
Those priests of his onto the wall?

The blood streamed into the sea. The fish fled.
Sublime dead miracle, trapped in the pupils of time.

Death with a falcon

The yellow sound of horns stabbing among the leaves,
Somebody's laughter dissolves in sunlight. The joy of thirst
Ripened in the saddle. Just before the clearing the branches
Unfold, like hands from eyes
In a capricious game. And then they saw:

A black bird hovering in a blue circle of sky.

Nobody smiles but the Despot, who knew.
Nobody but the Despot, whose face is furrowed
With a bloody wisdom, the Despot whose eyes
Are wide with remembrance, grey as the salt sand
Of swallowed time. The Despot lifts his gaze,
Slowly, like an over-heavy shield on a wounded arm.
And then he looses the falcon.

Later they said: the earth shook
When the bird disappeared and the Despot fell from his horse,
And the falcon kept circling and would not return.

If, in the end, one has to die, it is fine
To die with a falcon, one's own falcon,
Circling and looking for a black bird in a blue
Circle of sky, mad and blind with light.

from **Melissa**

Voices of the dead I

Voices of the dead. But not dead voices. Who
Can hear them? Rain on the copper gates of dawn. The cool
Of an overgrown garden, its nightingales held in a web of flowers.
I was the void between the lines, missing for hours

Down by the river, for days: it's all the same to me,
For this is a time outside this time, and the river is high
And wide. It flows with ancestral blood. But how am I
To swim upstream? Has anyone ever reached the sea?

O dead, upon the bank I found a house. With no
Rafters or roof-tree, abandoned in haste. And a thin thread
Of smoke was braided into the mist, which started to grow

Thicker. A half-built house. Then winter suddenly broke
And, frightened by the force of the storm, a window woke
Me. Who can hear their voices, the voices of the dead?

Morning

An age-old morning: the gods all show the same
Face in the caustic daybreak, immobile and cold,
All wet with others' tears, all green with mould,
Their smiles revealing beweaponed gums; no aim

To this morning – oh, the biting walls of this room
I must leave as usual to go among folk, to resume
Ancient migrations, with no hope of conclusion,
Through things whose presence, like stars, sows confusion;

A merciless morning, rain blue-voiced and raw
At the window, experience shackling my movements. While
Each morning I am weaker, the gods just smile

With their teeth; as I grow less, they stay the same:
Their cursed strength is my unknowing, this poor
Blood; my forgetting, these eyes, these hands that maim.

Slavery

O grubby god, my slavery to this voice,
This glass, this windowpane, this flower, this blade,
For the flower is only fire till it touches my hand,
The knife is a knife: outside me it's all arrayed.

O grubby god, my slavery to this voice,
To this hearing of mine which lags behind the real
Sound like a wounded hunter, mocked by a band
Of invisible birds, to these eyes of mine which wheel

As heavy as sunflowers, with their imperfection;
O slavery of presence, of learned motion,
Of mirrors and faces – time's fires burn

My bones, o grubby god, while my journey's direction,
Its sense, trails behind me like the ocean,
Embroidered with roses of foam, behind the stern.

The flower of beginning

And still, Melissa, you smile your thousand smiles from the bright
Gardens loud with bees behind my hearing, where grow
Your great transparent hives, thick with the honey of light,
Bitter with oblivion; where gyres, huge and slow,

A bitter sun through memory's dark sky, a sun
Which brings a purer waking, which brings still purer dreams
Than the dreams and waking of this death; o heavy honey-
Comb of ancient sense, which nowadays only gleams

For an instant, between the blades of fear, just like the toll
Of a bell whose clapper has been wrenched away, an old
Sound which travels on alone, forgotten but whole –

It is the voice of a bee, Melissa, buzzing gold
On a flower fresh as genesis, wet with morning rain,
Unfurling its petals beyond a sky of dust and pain.

The Argonauts

The sea let us be, engrossed with the eternity
In herself; and so we sailed, from shore
To shore, for days, for nights, for years.

The loveliest shores, of course, we left untouched –
Except for unravelled threads of scent borne on the wind
From vast orchards at the ends of the earth,

Beyond the path of our sailing; and yet
We learnt love and death, and a little sense,
Hard grains of gold in the sand of memory;

Yes, and the pride of adventure, defiled with blood
And washed in clean winds, beneath the stars
Where we clumsily wrote our names.

We came back, in the end, to where we began;
The crew scattered like a necklace: our destiny's thread
Had snapped. The captain crushed by the ship's prow.

The sea was still the same. Everything was still the same.
The ship, ribs blossoming open, lies rotting on the starting shore,
But few know the secret:
                          the end does not matter,

What matters is only the sailing.

Marina

My form, between this stone and a fruit
Ripened to flesh dark with the foam of a sun
Trapped between two similar flashes of death,

My form, a stranger to its source, most similar of all
To a sound clothed in the water I name:
Sea, fleshy shell of red fire;

My form, most similar of all to the dull green silver
Of the wind, which is etched with glittering images
And with a heavy sun, hollow bitter honeycomb

Buzzing with time beweaponed and winged;
My form, unrepeatable now, yesterday unremembered,
Tomorrow unknown, just as indestructible,

Bound to this sun with salty dark threads of blood,
As battered ships are moored
To a yellow breakwater, between two voyages;

It won't open to a bullet, won't open to a knife,
And slips between your fingers, like water,
And when you squeeze the fruit, you hear the sound of the tree,

You hear the sound of the sea.

Three squalls of rain

Time between lovers cannot be repeated,
Like the ratio of rain to sun in the flesh of this fruit:
Think of this while the rising bora, still an innocuous breeze,
Basks like lichen on the warm skin of the sea,
Because the year is aiming the sting of autumn at itself,
Emperor scorpion in the fiery ring of its form.

In the first squall of rain you'll recognise my voice;
In the second, you'll recognise your tears,
And the seed of a stronger wind's vine.

Time between you and me cannot be repeated,
And this night as it passes, shattered into Istrian stars
And bitter with summer's defeat, can no more be repeated
Than the motion of the flame imprinted lightly into the mirror:
Think of this, marooned in rooms of blood
Whose doors are slamming in an unknown wind.

In the first squall of rain a bird will still be singing;
In the second, the overgrown orchards
Fringing your sleep will burst into flame.

Hands are turned towards you, like gardens towards the south,
Inscribed with a map of memory: this is the line of the summer,
And this the star of the sea; this is the imprint of the eye
I press to the keyhole of your sleep
To spy on myself, to see myself smile
Strangled by the bitter vine sprouting from your lap.

In the first squall of rain this sea will grow dark;
In the second, you'll know your tears
At your loneliness's peak.

Who else but lovers, fused in a movement of defence,
Clasped together like a shell about a core
Incandescent with the bloody glow of a moment's sun,
Can plunge into a sea of death disguised as time
Only to surface the stronger, drenched in the sense of their blood,
And find eternity's seed when they open their embrace, like a fruit?

In the first squall of rain you'll recognise my voice;
In the second, you'll recognise your years
In the fiery ring of your form.

And this night which divides us cannot be repeated
In all the scenarios we write, with the pride of love,
With the fiery pencil of fear and desire,
Across the walls, across the bare water, across the years:
This night is growing into a rider and galloping past us,
Time between lovers cannot be repeated.

In the first squall of rain a bird will still be singing;
In the second, you'll recognise your tears;
We may not hear the third.

Love

For years I've been learning your features, where the days
Impress their tiny fires; for years I've been memorising
Their shimmering uniqueness, and the latticed lightness
Of your movements behind the net curtains
Of the afternoon; and so I no longer recognise you
Outside the memory which surrenders you to me,
And every day I find it harder to tame the current of time
Which does not flow through you, through the gentle metal
Of your blood;
            if you change, I surely change too,
And with us that world built around an instant
Like fruit around a kernel, woven of unreal flesh
With the taste of lightning, the taste of dust, the taste of years,
The taste of snow melting on the flame of your skin.

For years I've known that we are disappearing together:
You burnt through with the star of my memory, outside which
There's ever less of you, myself beautifully dispersed in you,
In every afternoon, in every room, in every day,
In everything which fills you slowly, like sand
Filling a riverbed;
            and this, our moment,
Lasts longer than another's death.

from Atlantis

> 'West of the Pillars of Hercules, an island bigger
> than Libya and Asia,' the Egyptian slowly told the
> astonished Solon, 'but it vanished in fire and water,
> in one night'.

Eye-witness report

This rock is no rock, it's a hill of memory
Slowly shifting in its bed and starting
To fall apart, the shape of ash eroded by rains
In which feral metal nightingales with broken wheels
Sing without sense or respite; a shifting hill
Filled with severed roots, like a corpse
In a pool of lapsed reasons;
The shape of ash from the burning of years
Once thought to be fireproof. This hill of memory, ash,
This rock, slowly shifting in its bed, is disappearing.

And was it memory, or just the brutal beauty of a time
Stronger than us in every second? On the sunbaked ridges,
Woods without leaves or bark: just a skeleton, picked clean
By insects and wind, is left of that pure summer
In reach of our ancestors' dream, our dream.
On the beach, the sea dissolves into vowels, free,
Unrelated to our meanings. We do not trust the sea.
Some fishermen set out, only to return burned,
With no skin, no blood, no memory. The sea is not safe.
This sea, its wounds sutured with the thread of stars.

Ships are already flying off the rim of a doubtful horizon
Into the void. Landslides tip gentle orchards

Down cracked slopes. Thin black swallows
With broken compass needles quivering in them
Circle brown oceans of sand until they vanish
Into the cruel air, like a meteor shower.
Water won't slake this thirst. On the table
Glasses shatter, caught by a stray tracer bullet of fear.
Was it memory that led us, or the brutal beauty
Of a time stronger than us, whose centre is giving way?

We have lit fires in the plains, and posted
Our sharpest-sighted archers on the forward shores.
High in the night, under the leprous face of the moon,
Rockets hum beyond the range of our age-old dream
That space can be tamed. But the archers are carefully taking aim
At your golden shadows, unborn inheritors of the earth.
At night, wet greylag geese loudly bypass our towns,
Frightened by the smell of our fear. The sea is rising.
This rock is no rock, it's a hill of memory
Slowly shifting in the pulp of the sea, and disappearing.

Love: a fragment

Love still lives on;
Beyond the thin membrane of blood stretched on a drum of fear,
Beyond the nights ringed by insomnia's razor wire,
Beyond the dry rivers, beyond the dust,
This rain, for instance, still lives on,
With the brief freshness of a fruit-filled year; love
Still lives on, proud and blind like an ancient bard,
Unfurled like a flag in the colour of a summer dress
Memorised on the floor, between the afternoon shadows.
Transparent ships still leave the jetties of breathless rooms
For the open sea of a sleep awash with fertility.
Mothers still bear children on a smiling wave
Of pain, heedless of what will ensue.

And children grow up on fractured coasts:
Inheritors of the earth, inheritors of water,
Inheritors of fire and air.

And yet the sea might be rising faster
Than the tender luminous seed inside them.

Tyrrhenian Sea

Beyond olive trees grey with the ash
Of a night charred by the tracer bullets of stars,
Beyond marshes rusty with grass, beyond leaning towers
And hills wet with the west wind –

The Tyrrhenian Sea,
                      a scented rag of blue
Torn apart by the thousand hooves of the sinewed air.

A flock of birds flies to meet us, a burst of buckshot
Peppering the rosy mortar on the low wall of morning;
In the fleshy leaves of figs ripens the bitterness
Of a rainy year, and the wind bears us the smell
Of dolphins axed to death on deck.

Towers lean over us carved in clouded ivory,
Dark towers of browned blood, rinsed long
In the gentle acid of the rains, and on them settles a flame
Wafted by the wind from splintered shores;
Rivers strangled with sweet sand decompose in the plain,
Between the crickets and the smoke signals
Of the Etrurian pines; the sea rises and slowly unfurls
Like a flag.

And if only we could stay here
Between the word *rain* and the word *tree* and the word *star*,
In this plain, between the hills, if only –

But you are already a little older, my love,
And this menacing world betrays us
And so keeps its balance,
                      one more day.

Inventory of moonlight

An Istrian moon
Stained with salt and the west wind,
Over the lean and dark green slopes
Gnawed by the feral air of the equinox,

A moon which might be a match
Lit in the stairwell of a Belgrade house
Razed to the ground sixteen years ago,

A house razed sixteen years ago,
A house inhabited by tainted fire and children
Who turned, as legend tells, into angels,

An angel, a smile emerging from the ashes
Like a leaf from a tree, defenceless;
An angel rehearsing a gesture on his wall
For centuries now, with unknown intent,

A gesture I make in sleep to ward off the birds
Fouling the wet carbide and singing like machine-guns
When, drenched in sweat, I want to wake in a garden,

A garden turned in compassion towards the sea
And steeped in the blue anaesthetic of afternoon shadows;
The old lace of light, yellowing and frayed,
And the fire of the sea between the trees,

A tree in the wind, already half fire,
A tree which seems to resemble the name
I've long been inventing for you, my love, in vain –

In a razed house, in dust, in wind,
In the years, in fire, gardens,
Yesterday, today, and tonight,
Lit like a match:

In the gnawing air of the equinox
Over the lean and dark green slopes,
Stained with salt and the west wind,
An Istrian moon.

Roman quartet

    I

Spring, the Piazza Navona trembles like a ship
Turning towards a trusted star, in a southerly wind,
Age-old, malarial and sweet.
                        Here I eavesdrop
Night after night on the stronger one inside me,
Comparing his heated voice, fogged by the breath of blood,
With the winged, haphazard words dressed in the voices
Of late lovers on the benches, this night of blind travellers
On the ship of my pride, sailing to the schedule of my death;
It was only this afternoon (after a shower of warm rain,
On the balustrade of that stairway ravaged by the fires of tiny
Flowers, above the roofs overgrown with gardens, with fruit,
With smoke and lemon-coloured light) that I believed
In you again, familiar, virgin world;
                                then night came,
Serene, inhuman, filled with the ultimate fantasy of fire
And bursting with another eternity, and overtook me
On the square in a fever of wind, a roaring of waters,
Listening in to the irresistible force which lifts me
From my blood like a wave, sets me sparkling,
Then scatters me.
                Yes, these relentless nights
Gouged by the stems of exploded stars,
Announced in the shattered tongues of fountains,
Strong on the black-green slopes of solemn pine,
Nights forever too big, forever overcrowded
With years of unknown intent; the strongest nights
Cause me to vanish all the faster, like a flame
Fed with the heady milk of the feral air, proud
To assert itself, condemned not to recognise itself
In times of fire and wind.

II

Mornings in the Via Statilia, as the wet, glittering voices
Of birds in the gardens opposite, already peeled bare,
Enter through the window like bullets of gentleness;
Quiet, phosphor mornings of love,

As the room blossoms into a hall of mirrors
Duplicating a single movement, or maybe the colour
Of a dress on a chair;
                        How come this transformation of a dream
Into the image of a world which exists, gentle, just for us,
Until we have set within it, like bright castings,
And morning falls away like a die, already cracked?

See – by day we are complete; or so we seem,
Like a statue voiceless until you smash it
And waken with fire the void and stars inside,
Scattering a recognised form proclaimed as purpose.
And this is your day:
                      these streets that glitter,
Accepting your footsteps like fate, fountains shot through
With sun, an espresso beneath the already dusty leaves
At an absurdly tiny table, a conversation about that star
On the Greek madonna's shoulder, and the stairway from where
I kept your smile, between the blossom and the barbarous
Clicking of cameras (*Say, Helen, what place is this?*);
I remember shop windows releasing your shadow
Like a leaf of copper and water; but where were you?
Perhaps you still lingered somewhere in the morning, or had fallen
Asleep at the first bullet of waking, which cannot quite kill
Your true face of fire,
                      my love.

III

That garden on the Aventine, before us and after the rain,
Brimful with air, laid waste by the beauty of the years,
Surely we'd been here before?
                              There were gates of glass
That you smashed with your smile, oblivious,
Happy and tired with walking; then water splashed
In a fountain, wet wings fluttered away, something rustled
In the cool, bristling pines. This garden existed,
Drawn with a sure hand on the map of time, beautiful
Before a sky the colour of morning sea-water
(Though it was afternoon, and the city all round us
Was peeling leaves of sun from its domes to expose
Its centuries, intimately, messily, like the wet washing
And gutted birds on the Campo dei Fiori,
A city effortlessly present, from one instant to the next).
And yet we couldn't quite believe this garden
Was real; it was all too close, too tailor-made
For us, and might all fall apart
At a word, a sudden move.
                          Even today I have my doubts
About that garden (as the wind doubts its name, the sea
Its taste), that garden slowly receding
And already starting to glimmer like a constellation
Orbiting an imagined year; a garden like a word
Spoken in love, and wafted away on the wind; a garden
On the Aventine, after us, before an unknown rain.

IV

It's time you were asleep, unknown lovers,
Whose faces night is tapping away at like a goldsmith,
Fashioning with a little fire a beauty he will forget.
Let this square, with its three fountains, be empty:
The air will knit together again over the space of your bodies,
As painlessly as lichen, as water. And don't look back:
All you know is already inside you.
                              And a strong night
Is coming like the sea, with no explanation or love.

It's time you were asleep, unknown lovers: woe betide
Those who stay awake, chained to the gates of the gardens
Of fire, as they used to chain tactless prophets.
It's time you were asleep, time to stop seeing
Your short shadows, to teach your blood
Obedience. See: one by one, the windows are burning out;
Behind them, the certainty of objects you love:
Lamp, bed, wall.
                And a strong night
Is coming like the sea, with no explanation or love.

Inhuman city, butchered beauty of duration, with velvet
Moths fluttering from your wounds, with swallows
Swarming at the intersections of your veins, city of wonders –
I will stay on alone, to see you renounce sleep, to see
A strong night, which makes me vanish all the faster,
Grow bitter with your name.
                            For there are places
Of last-ditch defence; sentries raise their voices
Like weapons and are dust, water and wind
Dismantle the glistening flesh of lovers, and yet
A star which returns must recognise something:
Otherwise it would not return.

from **Prolegomena to waking: shores**

1

For water's imagination to take the shape of a beast,
For wind to learn its first word,
For light to thicken, conceiving a bird
In its own image,

For the sea to feel it is,
For the sea to say freedom,
Its teeth needed breaking,
It needed naming;

Hence the creation of shores.

4

A space which thinks about itself
Notes its own vacillation,
Draws a decisive border –

And only then can the growth
Of hesitant voices begin, can the seed
Inhale air and flame,

Only then can an eye open one day
To the sight of a gentle sea
Reaping its blue
With sickles of light.

FROM
Act

Čin
1963

from **Algol**

    1

One water I remember: a leaf
Trembling like a hand on a horse's bare back;
A stream which set diadems between its reeds
Now cocooned in memory,
                          a wet butterfly
With two dark vowels for wings,

Or the water of sweat, or damp which opens upon the wall
The pallid landscape of a rainy summer
With trees of spongy fog,

Water in gentle hollows, like the evening sky,
Where the first salt crystals grow
Around invisible matrices of light,

And last of all, the water in my mother's milk, her blood –
Surely all I hoard in precious nouns,
In the silence after each defeat,
Surely this whole wealth of wetness

Cannot all cruelly evaporate,
Cannot be consumed, ashless,
In a single, sudden flash,
                      arrested
Like a bird before an unknown set of lenses,
Pressed like a stain
Into the bitter skin of some unknown sea?

The water I remember,
And all the voices
Glittering with dew like the metal of morning bridges?

3

Great, rainy summers
Where the trees are bright with a burly glitter,
And our ruined excursions, my love,
Somewhere in a space which still excites us
With its unrealised image:
                              a lake polished
Like marble, ornate with veins of light,
A clearing heaped with ozone between two rains,
A safe afternoon, shingled roofs
Washed and dried to the sheen of old silver;

And then the brief nights, which we remember
Fleshed on the frail skeleton of lightning
When we name each other, as if for the first time,
Beneath a window overgrown with shivering scales,

Or the rainstorm at night on the open street
With the naked voice of a bird
And chestnut leaves as heavy as nursing breasts:

Wet summers, beautiful stains in the rooms of the years,
Winds weighed down with raindrops,
If we don't manage to wish you farewell,
If we don't manage to wish you farewell…

4

I remember water, recall a star
Whose name I am afraid to say,

A star which could drink this world's water dry
In the delirium of an inconceivable thirst,
A star which this word cannot hold;

And all my words
Sling-shot into windy orbits
About an inconstant space in which I have squeezed
Love, and rebellion, and memory,
As the sea imprints its fires
On the seasons of the shores,

All my words, my speech,
My knife beneath the pillow, the glass of water on the table,
Images I barter for the right to pronounce them,
Names I slip as a bribe to time,
And birds I ring with the thin silver of memory,

All this might weaken
At the imposed moment of decision –

And so a star reminds me of silence,
A star shines over my book before I sleep.

Snowy night

Snowy night, onslaught of white purity, snowy night
Filled with the cold roe of sterile stars, yet
So ready to burst into flame:
                              in the violet branches
The treacherous substance of time, hidden and sinister,
In the bird's feather, in the blizzard. Snowy night,
But ever fewer words for the final defence,
For resistance to the splendid drumming of senselessness –

And now I mistrust the word *bird*, it will fly away,
Mistrust the word *water*, it will evaporate,
The word *wind*, the word *star*, the word *rain*,
The word *death*, with its all too lifelike gleam;

Ever fewer words, precious few perhaps,
For the moment of decision:
                              perhaps just two or three,
Huge, lost before they begin, upright
In the burning air – the only poem.

Will they be enough, wide world, my hard-won victory,
For me to protect you, defend you,
Extend you till the moment of truth?

Snowy night, flowers of white sulphur,
Foam on a wave of fire.

Winter letter

How strange you are when you're not here!
Between us, the air is choking on tiny flowers,
A snowstorm like a sweet disease. And when
My fingers touch you through the fence that rings
An ordinary dream, you start speaking, it seems,
Of things I do not know: a wisdom
Gold between two words, like summer air
Between two islands. But it is easier for me
To summon you in this way than to imagine
The space alleged to separate us (a night of violet salt,
A plain in whose silence I trace a straight line
Between the shrouded, starry woods –
A December night). Even if you're something else
Than all you know of yourself, on such a night
As this, when a sea, frightened by snow,
Opens and flutters like an eye in my blood;
Even if you are strange, my love, here where you are not,
Lit like a flame – look – on the candle of your name
In the empty room of the spoken.

So many ways to make me
Depend on you all the more!

Winter morning

> Winter has covered with snow… etc.
> VOJISLAV ILIĆ

After sleep as if after battle,
The flame of morning light fettered with tiny crystals,
Wind against the window, the thermometer's blue vein calcified;

The anatomical atlas of these gardens beneath the snow:
The invisible bloodstream of the potentials I foresee,
Chlorophyll roe frozen in time,
Flowers formed partly of vowels, partly of my blood,
The softest shadow of lungs, a bird flashing through a burst of rain –
All strewn with white ashes from the supreme fire;
Frozen milk and the morning paper, and seagulls,
Their compasses haywire, in the mists above Pelagonia,
Winged Anabasis with an uncertain outcome;

Caught in the radar net of the ache behind my forehead,
Somewhere far away, is the sea: the Twins, moving
Inside the blue-green womb of the deep.

March

Snow-covered hills suddenly all around us,
Icebergs in the light-blue sea of an afternoon
Bristling with leafless woods, white magnets
Fuzzy with needles –
                    tell me, where are we?
I remember a similar pattern of excitement
On a windless afternoon just like this, scarcely ruffled
From within (like the pond filled with an aspic light
Seeping from a drowned, still-moving rose of sun);

Look, sweet current of years, something
Is repeating itself, something unreasoned but kind,
Like a mother's unthinking kiss, like a phosphor word
Invented, forgotten and found in love,

Or the tears of a boy who is me, repeated in the swan
Beating its wings again and again on the edge
Of the frozen pond, and pasted into the spell
Of the afternoon sun –
                    and snow-covered hills,

Hills whose names I don't know, for they are beautiful and strange
In the ozone's invisible fires, in their slow stride
Away from this day, this terror, these words.

from Spring liturgy for a dead poet
(to Branko Miljković)

   1

Are you alone at last? Alone enough
To tell the earth: here is another name
For memory, for taste, for your despair
When forced to be a miracle in spring,
For all in you that turned into an echo
Beneath the fallen vaulting of this blood?
Alone enough to smile back at the fire
Of an uncharted star in orbit still
About that very centre where you stood
A day ago, but silence stands today?
Because you wished to be alone, and heavy
With that precise moment, to be alone
For just one night in which your blood and time
Merged quickly into one, like surging waters;

Are you alone at last? Alone enough
For you to show you're stronger than all beauty?
Or in the taste of reddish clay do you
Remember summer's mine of radiance,
And do you recognise the air above you
Alive with scattered signs, with words advancing
Upon you like some cruel grace, to strip
The brief peace from your eyebrows? Death, you see,
Lies outside the solution.
                          There's no sense
In calling to your angel with a silence
Hurled straight upwards like a falconer's cry,
Since every question is the same, the sea
Still roars through all the seasons, and the fires
Still take the same way down.

                                    And now it's time
For you to move on. All the voices in
The world are stretching upright in your hearing
And trembling on their long, thin stems. The wind
Will turn the page, as we repeat with you:
A poet's death supplies the evidence
That birds can fly and death does not exist.

4

Tree in the wind, held in memory as a letter
Whose word, like a lump of carbide, is about to blaze,
Tree in the wind, cast into lead which some typesetter
Prints in a sky almost illegible with haze,
Tree in a windswept landscape, sign of earth stripped bare,
O deaf-mute tree between the stalks of wheat and maize,
A crippled memory's signal: this hidden forgetting is where
The poem lives, the sea is born, the embers spark,
And where the first leaf, forming in the still-shaky air,
Mimics forgetting's star underneath the bark;
And where the world returns from forgetting, the world appears,
Tree in the wind, a cracked dawn's first written mark,
A bird sleeps in the sea, a word in children's tears –
And though the poem be clay, the poem is what one hears.

Even without false sparks, fire is fire, I'm sure:
It takes up arms in water, sand, forgetting's mazes,
Observatories fall, but still the stars endure,
The poem's ringed by silence, silence links its phrases –
And yet awareness follows, as spring follows fall,
Though it contracts like a pupil when forgetting blazes,
And stops short like the sea at land's unhearing wall.
But at the end of every land, a sea is waking,
Announced beforehand by a damp breeze; the caul
Of deadened vision splits, as the first leaves are breaking
Into red flame, o tree in the wind, without recalling
That there's no start or end, stunned by the shape they are taking;
Letter in a word that some law is impassively scrawling,
Tree in the wind, you stutter while fertile rains are falling.

Whether or not it remembers, beauty will persist,
Beyond the dynamited rails, the road resumes,
Birds still go on flying, death does not exist,

And the greatest of mistakes is the mistake of tombs;
Tree in the wind, sign of a stronger earth, your bare
Branch will leaf, like a flag on a lookout post that looms
Above a decided battle: your accent's changed by air,
Your roots feed on a bedrock of forgetting, and prise
It open; each spring confirms the land-ringed ocean where,
Beyond the deafest boulders, waking seas now rise,
Around its blazing nest the bird writes rings of flight,
Tree in the wind, word which makes your moment wise:
Look, beauty is coming back in hordes, and at night
The sea glitters with stars, the sea glitters with light!

Young woman from Pompeii

I shrank down like the pupil of an eye
Adapting too late to that cruel glare;
Already on the ground, I leant my burned
Forehead against my arm.
                            And then, my name
Disintegrated even faster than
My tender flesh, in clotted bitterness.
I forgot how to count, to breathe, to turn,
To look behind. I was an emptiness,
I was the dark cloud of my movement, just
A bubble in a sea of dead fire. Thus
I waited for the wet clay's slimy touch
To fill me without passion, as when water
Fills someone's footprint on deserted sands.

And now what do you know about me? Barely
Something about my brief wish to outlive
Myself, no more than a gesture, perhaps
Of weeping, and a shape sealed hastily,
Without intent. So how can I tell you
That there exists a domain where I am
More real than the voice attempting to
Imprison me, more solid than the light
In which you look at me? You think you know me?
Go on then, touch this shoulder: I'm not here.
However, my touch is much lighter:
                            there –
You are not who you were just now. I know you
And burn on your shoulder, before the fire,
The ash, before and after everything.

Places we love

Places we love exist only through us,
Space destroyed is only illusion in the constancy of time,
Places we love we can never leave,
Places we love together, together, together,

And is this room really a room, or an embrace,
And what is beneath the window: a street or years?
And the window is only the imprint left by
The first rain we understood, returning endlessly,

And this wall does not define the room, but perhaps the night
Your son began to move in your sleeping blood,
A son like a butterfly of flame in your hall of mirrors,
The night you were frightened by your own light,

And this door leads into any afternoon
Which outlives it, forever peopled
With your casual movements, as you stepped,
Like fire into copper, into my only memory;

When you go, space closes over like water behind you,
Do not look back: there is nothing outside you,
Space is only time visible in a different way,
Places we love we can never leave.

Aosta

Solstice in the high hills, clear fires
Printed on the young skin of summer, vultures
Hatching in roses of air, cataracts
Of smoky silver oxidising on the slopes
Between the flowers and bright tatters of wind on the pines,
The lichen of rain on the ridges: I listen to you,

To these pictures kept for the slim possibility
That I might recreate a world for you; the imprint of desire
Lives in the air, the imprint of a finger on a postcard,
Look, this is a moment when no place is untainted
With our exquisite blood; I dreamt about sparks of flowers
Burning through the snow, I dreamt about your name, I love,

In a glacier the colour of emerald and milk sleeps a creature
With a broken spine, and stone, and a restless tree of water
Twitches its bare roots; an unremarkable memory darkens with desire
As film darkens with light, now you are far away and legible;
For you, I'm saving this day full of hills, that start of summer –
For me, that blurred snapshot of love's other side.

In praise of the poem

Words that finally slam into silence
Like bullets into the plaster of a wall:
The rustle of sand as it trickles from each cavity, at whose base
Metal has crumpled to a flower in its effort not to stop;

And yet the wall is thicker,
And yet the wall has not stayed the same,

A bird which sings before dawn,
Deceived by the blaze of burning trees, and yet bears witness to light –

This constant act of recognition
Frustrated by misunderstanding,
Enabled by misunderstanding.

Belgrade Airport, June

A young beast emerges from the haze,
Slender metal muscles in a blaze of blue,
Sound condensed through a clouded lens, fire out loud,

And on the café terrace a few flowers, a little wind, unease
Like a harness-bell in the ringing glasses, where ice
Painlessly loses its sharp transparent edges, like a word
Defused in the sweetness of use;

Look, down it comes,

And I'll tell you again –
                              travellers live in illusion,
Nothing happened while they were dreaming
Under the anaesthetic of the upper abyss, distorted
In the concave chalice of afternoon, riders
Of the arrow's shadow:

Their imprecise measure defines everything still,

And the beast breathes on the clear runway, as if after a love
Which has no consequences.

Continent

Orchards in the wind, while blood-spattered sugar
Slips into a sea of lava along the pure abscissa of morning;
A rider of rain, of wind, of silver,
Is walled into the ordinate;
                            a swish of wings in the air,
Unknown minerals and the chill of yesteryear's snows
Mingled with flowers in rifts in the hills, a scent
In the wake of migrating birds, like the furrow of foam
Boiling up behind a ship;
                        your land, love,
Built around a word, a memory, like a ship
Around golden sections; the land which trembles
In this drop of ink, this drop of blood –

A continent still damp with the first morning's fog
Does not know we are dreaming it, in each other's arms.

Marina II

Let us stay a while
In this silence before a pure wrath
Which will not break, since it is already in us
Like lightning in the bitter blood of sea, like a wild seed
In the red dust I spit upon to knead into a god,
Into a wild rose, the dream of a white-hot bee
With a sterile sting of diamond,

In this silence on the shore,
This recollection whose echo seeps through the stone
From within, like sweat, here where blossoms of foam shiver
On the edge of flotsam, sleep on the sea's lashes
Heavy with salt for all the wounds in the world;

Look, a bird's skeleton still bewitched with the symmetry of flight,
Empty tin cans, metal embroidered with roses of rust
Like a thin veil with blood from a face –

Just a few scattered signs
And our voices mingling like blood,
Like the smells of lovers, like history;

Rebel words which emerge like stars
At the right, the predicted point.

from **Nereid**

    3

In the motionless air, the limestone wing
Flakes as far as the curdled glint
Of a sea of engine oil, emerald and glass;

I cannot know all that you might do,
Open as you are at every moment,
Machine invented to rust and build yourself,
You whose wet and starry shrewdness challenges me

To throw a stone, addressing you in your own tongue –
But you change again,
                       and the imprecise word is already dispersing
Like the brief rose of foam after the stone.

5

The night you're brushed by lightning, purer
Even than you, than the milky horror
Soon to silt up the mirrors of your blood,

The horror which feeds the huge, luminous sea-urchins
Huddled in the pines above your sleeplessness,

The night you're brushed by lightning, just to remind you
Of the terrible balance which rules you too,
Beauty with bitter palates of pearl

Which you'll shape by morning into blossom, into splinters
Whetted with stubborn gentleness, spattered with weary foam.

FROM
Circle

Krug

1968

Tomb in Prague

Frozen earth, every winter, and fingers of snow on the stone,
Judah Loew ben Bezalel scattered across the dust
Like a syllable from a ripped-up book;

Mercury, the first breath of fire, streaks of green
To Saturn, the black beginning;

A sky of lead and silver over Prague,
Crystals of wind above the Vltava bend,
The Rabbi slowly dissolving in the alembic of legend –
But the moment returns, without exception;

Jupiter, road from black to blue
Paved with opals of fire: the planets still sing
In the formulae, their gardens of glass;

In the end, nothing's impossible: words travel, like stars,
Wiser with every return, but also wanting to know more;
The dust of the cemetery glitters, there's the scent of invisible
Frost-flowers on the skin of air;

Sulphur, quicksilver, arsenic, plus something else
Measured, forgotten, promised.

Only a shadow of your truth, Rabbi Loew;
Blood shines like a ruby in the frozen earth – but
A passer-by places a pebble on your tomb, then leaves
With the snow, with the wind in the street.

Mozart

The region behind the mirror, deep blue
With the dregs of all the rains I've heard;
Hills overgrown with a pelt of silence
Dappled with the red-brown ash of stars –

The road is longer than expected,
The exhausted horses, whipped and sweat-flecked,
Come to a halt and whinny; in their nostrils the wind
Deposits the bitter pollen of asphodels;

The shadows of birds trapped in the crystal
Of a lasting moment,
                I listen,
The spindle hums as it reels the lightning in,

The guide smiles behind his golden mask;
We must be past half-way; the path
Drops steeply,
                the spindle spins –

Now I remember everything, and know the words
Present since the beginning, like the air
Between music and death.

Skopje's monologue

    1

My waking is clearer, my tissue is thinner,
My ashes are brighter: they mingle more readily
With the colour of air, with mortar, with a bitter wind;

And you say: who's that waking me? You prise out the words,
Maybe still in sleep, and your voice travels through stone,
Look, it's climbing through the clay, through the black silver of water;

Like a flower on its way from the seed to itself,
Your voice already formed, your whisper a shriek in me,
Your voice seeks out my air, slams against my moment

While I'm building on sand, burning in the rain,
My voice a twitter in you, my dream unknown in you –
Your voice razes my city, stops my clock,

And our times merge right here, where blood merges
With dust, right here, where walls crumble
On morning lovers, on a breath, on a glass of water;

Afterwards, the birds keep wheeling, filled with you.

2

The summer has passed, I've buried my dead
In shallow trenches on the hillside. Now the rain is trickling,
Dissolving them through the gravel.
                              I've set fire to the dead,

A misty, wet constellation high above
Your sleep, I've thrust them like the larvae of stars
Into your skin.
                  Autumn has come, the nights are longer,
I've mended the clock and I measure my time.

My time seeps into the streets again, like water
Into the desert. I've washed away the blood, I raise stone
On stone, erecting words letter by letter
In air that tastes of the first frost.

My tissue is thinner, my ashes are brighter,
But my sleep is easier
And memory tougher.

Waking, one winter night

Is it time? The sea lifting these heavy eyelids from sleep,
Matted with golden dust from phantom orchards?
Is that a falcon perching on this outstretched arm,
A twig of fire in its beak? The palimpsest peeling like
An evening sky, the letters already shining through?
No, it's the window startled by a wind in gloves of snow,

The clock ticks the attack of snow's antlike voices
As sleep, from its fall-back line, still prints behind the eyelids
The shadows of images shrivelled to illegible letters,
Then disbands; far beyond sight the hum of orchards,
The swell of the sea, far beyond a sight that's peeling to raw
Skin in a winter room at night. And now the falcon

Drops its twig of fire, yet again. What falcon? Waking
Is home to forgetting, amnesia to snow's pure voices
Beneath the black dome of air. The night is peeling like
A wax rose, hour by hour, as the wind rattles the shutters
Of a demolished house in memory, and the branches
Of orchards in this same night of snow, and scatters the letters,

A syllable from a disbanded sentence, just some harmless
Letters, but the falcon stabs the falconer with its beak
As he lies asleep in the humming gold of the orchards –
Yet it fails to wake him in this night of wind and snow
As the clock beside him shackles his eyelids to the gaze
Waiting for morning to peel the night from the window.

Now ice is shackling the river, is peeling its flow with a knife
From thick stalks of wind. Trees in the snow like letters.
And if sleep descends on these ever-heavier eyelids,

It will be blacker than a night which knows no falcon,
And emptier than a night of pure wind and snow,
A sleep from the far side of dreaming, a sleep with no orchards.

Because it's only once a night, a night of phantom orchards,
That you wonder: Is it time? And the palimpsest peels
Beneath the knife of the same flame that imagines the shape
Of flowers under this snow, and calls out the letters;
It's only once a night that the falcon recognises its arm,
It's only once a night that the sea lifts its eyelids,

The sea lifts its eyelids matted with the gold of orchards,
A falcon wants to perch on this arm, the cocoon peels –
O all you scattered letters, you pure voices of snow…

Lyric

This spring is on your loom, Penelope;
Your fingers frozen and swift, your silver knife
In the threads of rain, in the rags of wind,
In my memory of a summer dress,
Of the movement opening it as light opens a flower –
Why do you unravel that pattern,

How will you repeat the design of spring, this task
Already disturbed by your game of patience?
The decision is not in your fingers,

And only the pattern on the loom falls victim.
You will repeat it clumsily and without love;
At dawn, frost is on the peach blossom
Like salt on a wound,
                            and the air in the room
Blue with sleeplessness.

from **Love in July**

    2

A taste of storm in the stem of the invisible rose
You absently twirl between your fingers;
A summer of black and gold,

But there is no wind, and rain
Glistens only on your words, like phosphor
Along the seams of water;
A summer of black and gold,

And lightning, which travels more slowly than memory,
Will never shine upon us in the same place twice,

Lightning still heaped with flowers and snows,
Somewhere on its journey round the year –

A taste of rain on your lips,
A summer of black and gold.

Orange
(for Dobriša Cesarić)

The water and the earth, the fire and air
Inside this perfect fruit last till they bear
Flesh: the moment of ripeness that's their goal.

Revolving slowly through the chilly leaves,
A stellar system.
     Autumn.
        Being whole.

Photographs: a romance

That weightless boy, abruptly shackled, kept
In memory when he'd hoped to fade to air;
That gaze, a stinging lash of sea-spray swept
Across the trembling membrane between there
And here, that form long filled by winds, long slept,

That gesture – look – arrested in its space,
Its flash, now out of joint, from long before
Returns flat, legible, inscribed with place
And season, like a theatre bill; the law
Which states that everything's a special case;

That time, a tape-loop snipped out by the Parca,
Her scissors by the reel, that music – listen –
Of memory woven in with something darker
As ozone smokes and silver fish-scales glisten,
That moment which returns as its own marker,

Alive and yet debased in its new shape, a
Drop in a downpour with nowhere to flow;
That boundless ocean turning into vapour
As time keeps smiling, feeling itself grow
Denser, till all things shift to prints on paper –

Those drifting spores which glitter in the beam
Of someone's gaze, those acts nipped in the bud;
Those ghosts, a woman's and a sea's, both gleam
Without a drop of their beginnings' blood,
That windblown pine, a smudge in its own dream –

Yet, terrifyingly, perhaps, there's more,
That boy who keeps on smiling weightlessly;
Yet, terrifyingly perhaps, there's more,
That gesture slipping from its axle-tree;
Yet, terrifyingly, perhaps there's more,

That laughing face, that time which has recurred
But wants to stay just like it was back there
Before it clotted in a flash, unblurred,
Back on the far side of this lethal air,
That flicker in the eye of a stuffed bird –

Phantoms! Small ads of silence! All those raw
Imprints of a measure which domineers
This sureness saturated with the law
Of blood, the law of motion and of tears,
Imprints of a measure which will endure;

Winged stars, and seeds! Those wishing to hear none
Of these reports about your mission know
They can no longer dream of being one;
On the far side the testimonies grow,
The world takes shape till, piece by piece, it's done:

That time which, like a snake, sloughs off its shell,
Its caul of glassy scales, in this same breath
Of wind which drives my words to sprout and swell
Between the narrow crevices of death,
That boy who smiles is me: I know him well.

Joanna from Ravenna

    1

Ship on the sea, bird on the runway of wind,
Joanna between the petals of gold
In the marshes, with rain and wind and sun,

Joanna, sister of the years and the towers
Heavy with wind, leaning into the mud;
Joanna, sister of the star returning
Over the gentle skin of melted snow,
Joanna, sister of the will-o'-the-wisp –

Joanna wrapped in the scales of her gown,
With a smile smouldering among the gold
Amid the teeming of hard and shiny insects buzzing
Green like the ring on her finger;
Her eyes are two immemorial midnight seas,
All their depth distilled into two droplets.

Joanna, a fixed star; and rain
Coming from the ocean to her window;
A star fettered with the tongue of death,
Joanna breathes, Joanna smiles.

2

Ship on the sea, lightning in the year,
Dam in the hills, the humming of a turbine;
Joanna, sister of time, glitters on.

These words remember her. This wind
Lashing the window with late winter snow
Last summer touched her eyes,
Lips and hand, and her emerald ring.
And now, as I write her name,
Joanna listens to the pen, glitters on.

Joanna between the petals of gold
With a smile smouldering like phosphor
Listens to the swell of the sea, the flash of a bird,
The turning of a turbine before the dam bursts,
And to these words which will touch her

With the fingers of my fire, after me.

from **Dubrovnik, a winter's tale**

The masons

The measure is in the stone, and the tongue of earth is crushed
In the voices of chisels, seeking each other
In the echo of dust, like children's voices
Between the raindrops;
                          sometimes we recognised
A scream or a word, trapped it,
Set it upright in air. We found the measure of walls,
The weeping of crenellations, the smile and the vine,
The movement of a beast rising from the stone
Like a star from the sea: innocent, washed clean –

We measured the stone with a yard of iron,
With our imperfect love;
                          we translated
An unknown tongue into known forms,
And celebrated that unspoken agreement
With the stronger measure of substance;

Then the earth shook –

Somewhere there had been a mistake,
                                  unclear even in the flash
Of dust settling, of the tongue melting
Into its genesis, like water;

When the blood was dry
We tried again.

Portal: pietà

You're slipping from my knees, century by century,
But we stay in this balance, imperfect
On the surface of a perfect grief, like oil
On water.
          Footsteps beneath us
And a door the colour of bile and tar,
Voices, words and years
In their unrepeatable similarity, from moment
To moment. So we are frozen
In a stone pivot of pain, raised above
The continuation of fate, shackled
To the borderline of love between stone and iron –

And beneath the merciful rains,
Beneath the gentle filth of pigeons,
We darken like the back of a mirror
Turned towards emptiness.

The Dark Province

Murmurs crumble with the crunch of gravel
In the long tunnel,
                      cracked hooves clatter,
We hold on to each other's voices and shoulders
In the darkness of the final world;
                                  drops of light seep through,
A wick fed with the thin oil of memory, another,
We ride beneath the roots, beneath the years,
We share our ration of bitter poppies with the hungry shades,
Our faces frighten us, from afar, at the exit.

Somewhere here all paths cross
Before their final parting, and the track of the beast is confused
With the track of the angel at the still, terrible centre:
If you stay you'll regret it,
If you go you'll regret it.

FROM
Of the Works of Love, or Byzantium

O delima ljubavi, ili Vizantija

1969

Of the works of love

The works of love are scattered through the world
Like the scars of war;
      but grass grows fast
Over the battlefield, and the wet embers of earth
Burst into flame to restore the terrible virginity,
As before the embrace, before the remembering,
Before the voices at dawn, with lips just parting:
The works of love are in dispute –

And when the wall crumbles, when the garden grows wild,
When the word is erased, when the ring breaks,
Love loses out;
      but listen to the screams of the birds
Over the cove where lovers teach the sea
A different tenderness: time is impartial,
And the world is love's task,
        the long rehearsal
Of immature gods.

Memory of an orchard

Don't forget that orchard, Melissa, the orchard
On the tumbling slope of a summer already ages old,
Like a word the instant you say it;
                                  the orchard
Was picked bare: only a few late fruits ripened
Between the dark, flickering leaves dry at the edges –
Fire had changed direction.
                         We spoke in a language
Like water: quick on the surface,
Sparkling and sweet to a thirsty memory.
                                       It's strange
How fate unpacks the makings of our past, for us,
For future remembering: now I recall your gesture,
Your hand outstretched for a random gift – an unthinking,
Irrevocable testament. Evening fell quickly:
The smoke of smouldering branches, the milky drop of a star;
As we left, you walked just a step ahead of me
Through an orchard suddenly heavy with all the fruit of earth
Which no one picks,
                  whose taste is unknown.

* * *

Then you may have said:
      'But still I think
The most beautiful thing is what we love with an inkling
In our soul', unaware you were repeating yourself,
That you were a mirror of a sister's lips
Eaten away by the sea in some ancient apple-grove of spray;
I heard you merged with the voices of waves, with
The invisible silver which sings on cicadas' wings
In afternoon hordes;
     or then you may have
Said nothing: it's all the same. In a clear time
Everything is already uttered, and the space
Between word and deed, between fire and rose, is repealed,
And misfortune ruled out:
       this is where I listen to you
Tonight, as September's gaudy flame consumes the summer
In the whispering woods, and the familiar stars depart
Once more, like armies, for their winter quarters.

The sea described from memory

Space, hollowed out by rain's lost needles
And clear between the pines: a blue move of silver,
With every possibility assembled like an army
For the brief festival of an image;
                                           but up on the scarp
Children's voices fill the air with time, and water
Hisses between the rocks, wave repeats wave,
A boat's keel ploughs the shingle of the cove;
There is no whole: it's terribly far to the centre
Of this tranquil power, its edges overgrown with lace –
Only a kinship of images, remembered deep in the soul,
Still sings a service to its source:
The dry snow of olive-groves, the moon in a quarry,
A pomegranate, crimson inside like the earth,
A pool of ink from the chronicle of the stars –

So that much later, in some winter's room,
A beast, silver and blue, may rise
In the ear's draughty labyrinth: the sea.

Song of the statue in the earth

In another garden, my face,
Just invented, is slowly turning
Towards a preciser pattern of stars;
                                     here
I no longer have a face: the back of my head smiles
At the wrath of earth, the labour of darkness
In my lobeless ear;
                   the wind
Which blows from the future does not move
The roots around me, the heavy wings
Of an angel grounded for the moment
A higher light lasts;
                   o leaves,
Thousand eyelids in motion!
And the roots slip away from me
And a drop of rain trickles down my shoulder
Which an unknown hand is already touching
In another garden.

Byzantium VII

One day, under the wise escort of our ghosts, someone
Might walk along the contour of these battlements, where
We watched the sun, a copper weight tilting into the scale of night;
The sea will leach silver and flotsam onto the pebbles
Rounded with future gentleness; the air will be blue
With the smoke of our names;
                                     but who will understand us?
For the centre will have shifted, the images will be different,
Perhaps now linked to a stem: perhaps a flower –
And the works of love be linked into a speech, a tongue;
But who then will wish to assemble our testimony
From these scattered syllables, from the cries
Caught by chance in some antique mirror,
In the surge of a wave? And why?
Will there be room tomorrow for this babel
In the serene memory of some angel, in the smooth memory
Of young waters? The memory of lovers?
Will anyone need the betrayed images of our love,
And the sentinels out in the desert with sand in their lungs,
Will anyone need that meagre tongue of misfortune,
Maturity's swift penalty, sentenced to defeat?
Or will the balance be more exact without us,
And the tongue of lovers sweeter without our voices
Mingled with death as the wind with flame,
As the source with the sea?

FROM
Fading Contact

Smetnje na vezama

1975

Winter sea

A winter sea white with fresh scars,
After-images of summer shivering in the pines,
Say something, if only to voice
The root of a rose –
                      you know
The unfinished returns like justice,
The imperfect must pass away –

Everything you do becomes a reply,
Every wrong word infringes memory,
Hesitation annuls it;
Say something, voice
This moment: quickly, the rose is budding,
The air condensing ready for the blossom,
The tongue bleeding on the word thorn –

(We walk down the path towards the shore
Between yesterday's images, real only today
In our speech, where souls
Touch like leaves in the wind…)

Marina V

In the acetylene flash of lightning (the lumbering thunder
Lags behind, can't keep up with the picture)
A drystone wall, a fig tree, a white pelt, the phantom of the sea –
In an illuminated arc, the storm skirts
The moment anxiously remembered
With unknown intent;
      then a sigh
In the darkness after the image, from the sea below
(Just one enormous tear
On God's stony lashes),
But not a single star shines through;
        on the extinguished headland
A red point ignites and dies
Like a fag-end tossed into the water,
      then flares
Again, the spacing regular
And each interval of trepidation
Enough for a birth or a death:
Without light, the sea is disarmed,
The sea has no future.

Genius loci

If you rehearse long enough the art of return
To the self-same place,
                        which finally starts
To remember you, like some stubborn coincidence,

If you return long enough to grow old in the shade
Of the same, more lasting image,
Don't be surprised to hear the splash of water
In the chill of a cistern, the fleshed lightning of an eel,
The death of a wet insect (though you know full well
That in the cistern is dust, crumbling walls,
And a sloughed snakeskin),
                            for wisdom here is older
Than illusion: strange, at times, are the rewards
For faithfulness to things less quick to change –
In the cleft of the snake's tongue, time quivers
And slips back into itself;
                      and so you become
Clairvoyant in one compassionate direction, towards
The gleam of an image which has no memory of you:
Look how the sea shimmers through the thinning pines –

The sole blessing of a place you love.

Fiesole, rain

Perhaps part of the landscape will stay forever
In your keeping: evening already visible
On the bright edge of cloud, like the trace of a lip
On glass;
         and then the legible upright
Handwriting of gardens on the hill terraces,
The beginnings of rain opening the air
From the scented side, somewhere near –

Images after love, it's true, are wedded
More beautifully with those to come:
And so I recognise that moment
As it vanishes, pure, bright and even,
Like a wished-for fate, like ice in a glass.

Belgrade from old photographs

    1

A varnished wooden box the colour of wild honey,
On a water-strider's long segmented legs,
Glitters its greedy Cyclopean eye,
Swallows weeds and couch-grass, swallows
The tiles of a roof on the Sava slope, chews through
The river just before it joins the Danube
Along with the memory of a rainstorm
In the marshy plain across the water –
Lichen on the wet bricks of the citadel
Plots the shape of gardens in a space wiped clean
(*And sporting a hat modishly white*);
The time on the Clock Tower recedes, like a star,
As you turn the page where it is the print of a print
Of an April light that still smells
Of quicklime, pitchpine, gunpowder,
Of air riddled with hope –
And so you witness the birth of geometry
On the Danube slope: palings and mud,
Maybe even *The scent of lime trees from gentle Vračar*
In that speeded-up motion
Where the two-legged shadows stay glued
To the cobbles' dusty instant, anonymously,
Like flies to a windscreen;
                              but
At the Scales, where stone lions
Spew a healthy silver, no measure is certain:
Just downhill, a bare-headed Prince hoists himself
Into the saddle, 1882, his bronze hand pointing
Across the set, into the wings already

Being eaten away by yesterday's air,
                              one molecule of which
Is wedded to the blood of the hand
That turns the page: this is how history
Merges with memory, as the Danube with the Sava;
Now try to turn the pages
Back –
         ash is left on your fingers.

2

But there's still the possibility
Of real continuation: of writing on
In the book that others have compiled for us –
Of peeling a forgotten light
From the Cyclops' retina;
                         of stepping
Once again into a tram at the Scales,
Thus tipping the balance between yesterday
And tomorrow with the drachm
Of today's memory;
                      of crossing the bridge
Suspended once more just for the moment
Of crossing, real in the air of what was,
Over the Sava washing away into the rains –

Printed in countless copies,
This picture lives because it returns,
Similar and never precisely the same,
To recognise itself in an eye which ages
From inside, like a fruit in the shade;
                               and so
A future grows with every return.

3

In a fossil of light from 1865,
From the roof of a building just raised
By *Misha Anastasievitch To His Fatherland*,
You see a huge garden which you will never enter –
There is no flaming sword: the way is barred by the symmetry
Of space imagined to pass like time;
The honey scent of the tall lime trees is sealed
In urns and stored on the far side of memory;
From this direction the world is shut tight: there's not a crack
For a knife-blade, or even the flat heart of a lime-leaf
To slide through;
                    but maybe you've managed
To get in through another picture, walk down to the Danube
Along someone else's line of sight, and spring the trap:
One detail in common, a seeming coincidence – yes,
Dreadnought Tower's still there, that column rising into sight
From the eight-sided cell of a bitter, ancient comb,
Between the trash, beside the gravel-box, beside the tracks;
The stone stem of a huge rose of air
Unfolding petal by petal, whose scent is time –
There you may have understood,
There you may have heard the wheel turning,
There you may have heard a rustle, the rustle of wings.

Cantico delle creature

The bones are dry in the coffin, in the cellar
Of cellars, where a dense toxic thicket
Of snuffling tapers stands weeping,
                                      and a fan,
Invisible, drums like the memory

Of an air raid –
We blink at the motley-coloured street
As we return across the ridge; in the middle of the afternoon
We suddenly feel night, her black seeds

In our nostrils; somewhere holm-oak is burning –
Pilgrims come towards us
(Brother wind, sister water and brother fire)

Blossoming with leprous sores:
All that is left is the celebration of wrath,
Stern sister of an absent wisdom.

Letter to John Berryman
On hearing of his death

Dear friend (you gave me the right yourself – and not
So long ago, though immeasurably long
Ago for you – to address you in this way),
In one of our conversations about Hart
Crane, there lives the fact of his death, a death which
Resembles, to a certain extent, your own –
A leap into the water, when the instant
Is brimful with its own negative measure.
So permit me today, from your perspective,
To envy Crane, whose ending was one which left
No remainder: a leap in the night, over
The rail of a growling steamship, out into
The phosphorescent glittering of the waves
On the Gulf of Mexico; everything else
Is the poetics of the scale and measure
Of the moment when a poet died.
                                              Whereas
You were to choose your overarching moment
In the cold black water of a January
In Minneapolis (I know it well: ice
Lies upon the water like glass; and later,
The police, and the flash of the reporters'
Cameras, the newspaper headline: Professor's
Corpse Discovered… etcetera; your suit was wet,
The cloth a little gritty with ice, but your
Spectacles were left somewhere down in the mud).
Recently Celan, faced with a similar
Choice, opted for the Seine, one March or April –
He'd been a long time in the water, and
His body had none of those crystal edges

We find in his verse… And yet, these deaths are all
Too similar: the sickly-sweet singing of
Birds, terrible in the blasted tree of nerves,
The siren song of nightingales, or maybe
The nightingale song of sirens, monsters which
Come into being in order to mark out
The field for the final act, emptied at the
Instant when what edges our words is only
The flash from a feverishly imagined
Centre, shivering at its own solitude –

Now, I assume, everything's fine, and the price
Is less than Dante calculated (do
You still remember…?); but one calculation
Still remains: the weight of the unspoken words,
The ashes of a fire that did not burn – the
Debit side of a reply broken off by
The notion of leaping into cold, dirty,
Black waters – I understand the denial
Of the year's beginning, which, I must admit,
We celebrate whatever the price –
                                      but please
Understand me, you who succumbed at last to
Temptation, to the advantages of the
Shorter way: we all got more
                                      than we deserved –
Your courage is that of the prodigal; I
Respect it, but choose to admire the courage
Of those prepared to keep on giving answers

Even when the lips that question are silent.

from **Athos in five songs**

Daphne

Close to joy and hard to grasp,
Light woven in stone comes down
Between holm-oak and laurel
To where the landing stage opens
And a wet rope coiled round a bollard
Sings an age-old loyalty.

I tread the dust, which glitters
With a flake of flint, a fish-scale, the print
Of foot on foot (here begin the paths
Trodden by the same stride of hope
Into time immemorial); and it's simplest to say:
I recognise that stride, and the voices
Walled up forever in the column of air
Borne on my shoulders;
Recognition: surely my aim amounts to more than this?
Since the real reason for coming is loyalty
To an image pledged a moment ago, loyalty
To a word unspoken in the briefness of memory,
But whispered
In a future which brushes my cheeks
And parts the new leaves of the old plane trees
With the fingers of the same sea-wind
On this terribly real shore.

On the way to Esphigmenou

Later, perhaps when winter
Turns the cold lining of air and shifts our conversation,
Already gilded with the thin leaf of images,
Off to the north and into memory,
Perhaps the details may become a whole,
And chance be finally banished
To a space without words;
                               now we talk,
And everything is dangerously equal
In its uncertainty, in the burning sun
Nailing our shadows to our heels,
Dusty on the red path
Leading to Esphigmenou
Through the olives and the flowering broom –
Around the bend, the mother-of-pearl on a snake's back
Comes to life in a slow dance of retreat
Into the undergrowth, Saint John's wort
Blossoms out loud on the path; droplets of light
Seep through the membranes of bees' wings; to our left,
Between the cypresses, the view unravels
Into the sea's pure line, the monastery is a little further –

All that we accept without proof is only a pledge
Of future, of a more perfect memory:
The real effort is still to come,
The courage which perhaps begins
With the choice of the exact image,
                               with the touch
Of fingers feeling the edge of the remembered
In disbelief, like the edge of a wound…

Byzantium VIII, or Chilandari

The only track leads between blossoming olives
Older than many a city or truth;
In the thinning grey of the leaves the sea is far away
And as blue as the camera's eye:
If the picture turns out, it will have captured
My doubting of the miracle
Blurred into a smile, almost ghostlike –

Because the miracle actually happens round the next bend,
The miracle is a citadel with a single gate,
Where the password must stay unspoken without mistake
And one must enter at the proper hour, filled
With love for the visible:
                      for stone, brick, lead,
Towers, galleries, cupolas,
The silver foil of afternoon sun
On the thin glass of windows, for a shadow
Climbing, like oil up a wick, straight up the cypress
In the close paved with stone
And wild mallow –

For through the visible runs the border
Of joy from the other side – the measure of the given,
The only chance to change the ineffable
For ready coin, for divorced images
To meet: this is why miracles are confirmed
In the unremitting space of the seen, where a purple
Weeping lies on the letters, and the wind scatters
Needles of swallows across the folds of air
Over Saint Sava's Tower,
And moss is eating the lightning

Absorbed into the northern wall of Chilandari
Where, at night in my room, the glass of my oil-lamp
Takes the shape of a heart, and by that flame I write –

I write of the rose and the peach tree in the close,
Of compassionate eyes in the gold,
And reflect on the Supreme Master of love, bending
Over the perfect sketch of a miracle.

Mnemosyne

1

Autumn arrives like a slap in the face, on the threshold
Of September, in Aquileia: the wipers peel the rain
And squashed insects from the windscreen,
                                            we slow down:
So this is the town, this stone rowlock in the plain
Between the black cypresses creaking in the wind
Like the planks of a boat;
                        and the gnawed bones
Of a jetty drowned in wet grass,
Rain-soaked crickets, a few wild flowers,
The mosaic floor of yesterday's summer buried in ozone
Under the fallen vault of lightning; so we'll have to
Take their word for it: the signs, described
In the guidebook, the fragments, and the darkness
Beneath our feet, and the red sunshade in front of the cafe
Heavy with rain as Attila's tent
Three days before the slaughter, this is Aquileia –
This healed scar
And this name, a dried pericardium, silence
On which history floats like oil on water;
On our return, the quarter of sky to the west
Shines the colour of ice, of blue flame –
The screen switched on, but no picture.

2

Water is only a swifter image of earth,
Her sister in a different duration; hence
The city's founder, ploughing a furrow
For the solemn sowing of squares and towers, resembles
The boatman ploughing the water with his wooden prow,
Five miles an hour, with white weeds of foam
Growing over the furrow behind his stern;
                                            the difference,
Most obviously, lies in the speed
With which the scar heals over; it is in time,
And hence conditional; and yet, if I understand water,
Because I remember the reason for her innocence,
I do not understand earth, her work, the stubborn wrath
That eats the letters from the stone, hems
Any peaks protruding above her own slow wave,
Overturns the tombstone with a lime tree's root, wants
To smooth out the imprint of a long love, on her only bed –
When did the feud begin? And why?
We gather consequences, as the breeze
Gathers poppies along the road;
                                the storm thickens,
In the wind, the weathervanes are rattling,
                                        but
The movement's direction is quarrelling with its speed.

3

A trained eye can recognise the unhealed humus,
The traces of ramparts in this dusty Arcadia of tobacco
And the vine;
           from the shadow of a hill
The Acropolis has peeled like a scab;
                              a cicada's cry
Like barbed wire in the stunted fig tree –
Heraclea, in her horizontal darkness
Punched four-square into the foot of the hill:
In the shallow pit a little stone stubble,
Two lines of Hesiod mutilated like statues
And the afternoon sun slanting over the orchard of Eden
Conceived with the aid of tesserae, on the floor
Of a church since faded away;
                         cedar and sweet cherry
And pomegranate, fruits not pecked away
By the beaks of flame in the dark. Why not?
Is there a choice, is there an order
In the long migration of landscape into landscape, wall
Into emptiness, emptiness into tree, into shadow,
Shadow into hope, hope into wall? Anyway,
There's no clean future: space stays infected
With the fever of signs, the germ of remembering –
And a mother's kiss
Transmits the saving disease.

4

They eat forgetting with their bread, the blind who dream
Of a vacated future, swept clean like a room
Before the arrival of a new lodger;
                                    the rose of rust
Is already sewn into the steel girder which hovers
Over the building site, rain sketches a garden
And a network of streets in the desert, the rubbish heap
Moves down the river, the temple up the slope, the highway
Slides beneath the earth like a snake – movements are linked,
The word future only denotes the unfinished;
But terrible is the effort to recognise love
In the waning, and to read the sign
In the nettle between two syllables of stone, in the wound
Which heals more swiftly than the telling –
There is resistance from the beginning, earth trembles
In the sweat of dew, in effort, in light:
He who wrestled with an angel made
History in one night;
                          our task
Is to remember, to deliver blows;
The task of the peach is to blossom.

To sons growing up

Never again as closely in step
With the expressible, but without hesitation, my sons,
As now, your heels still winged with the
Short shadows of years;
                         look, the drawing book on the table
Contains a copy of reality, as yet unthreatened
From its uncertain frontiers, in a ball the sun's form
Confirms its closeness, and the summer's so long,
You say, and it's only just begun –

And so you help me to recall
Forgotten skills: how to be in balance
Yet heedless
Of the black scissors on the dial, cutting out
A piece of future memory (perhaps of forgetting,
The choice is still there),
Not how to test the visible, but how to believe
In a named object: pencil, flowerpot, wall…

But how can I tell you that danger lies
In speeding up wisely, in speeded-up wisdom,
In the merciless feud of image with image,
In the mirror's malignant, age-old disease
Of turning original forms the wrong way round?
That danger lies in the inevitable
Linking chance to chance
As water links the roots and grass of the world?

To state the danger, but to be
True to the visible: this is the real lesson;
I shout it into the wind that blows from the future,
Wafting back my ashes, and your voices.

FROM
The Passionate Measure

Strasna mera

1984

A note on poetics

Guarding the unspoken, like a core.
Learning this from the apple: earth, lime and rain
Work only towards the fruit, finding expression
In that imperfect but ripened sphere
Which you can't compare with a pear.
Rehearsing the art of renunciation.
Stamping out a spoor.

Standing in front of the mirror, unafraid of
The reflexive image: it returns the expression,
Imperfect at that, of abstraction's stubborn effort
To clothe itself in flesh,
In a good conductor of pain.

And yet, without hesitation,
Saying bread to bread, saying wine to wine,
And to the woman you love: I love you.

The spaces of hope

I have experienced the spaces of hope,
The spaces of a moderate mercy. Experienced
The places which suddenly set
Into a random form: a lilac garden,
A street in Florence, a morning room,
A sea smeared with silver before the storm,
Or a starless night lit only
By a book on the table. The spaces of hope
Are in time, and not linked into
A system of miracles or a unity;
They simply exist. As in Kanfanar,
At the railway station; wind in a wild vine
A quarter-century ago: one space of hope.
Another, set somewhere in the future,
Is already destroying the void around it,
Unclear but real. Probable.

In the spaces of hope light grows,
Free of charge, and voices are clearer,
Death has a beautiful shadow, the lilac blooms later,
But that's why it looks like its first-ever flower.

The raven's monologue

The dove, I believe, is a much better bird
For the job, for bearing, in its weary little beak,
News already condensed into a symbol,
Into a branch, a hope, a model for a painter
Postering peace. This is why I choose absence,
Now the springs of the deep and the floodgates
Of the heavens are closed. I choose clear-headedness:
Before me, the deluge. My black feathers carry the sun,
I shrewdly mind my own business, from under the ooze
I deftly pick out the eyes of sinners. I croak.
They will paint me on escutcheons, and standing
In the snow, black as a letter. They will teach me
To say Nevermore. I will be famous.
The dove, however, seems made for the job.
In its form may hope grow feathers,
In my feathers may horror gain form.

Elegy, or the Danube at Donji Milanovac

From the summit of Miroč tousled with forests
The river now seems like a sea, though it has merely
Slowed into a lake, for love of the generators
Humming downstream, gargantuan, greased;
We can't hear the wood-witch above the grind of the engine,
In second gear, down the hairpin bends deployed
Along the green contours. Our goal, Donji Milanovac,
Filled with roses, has moved uphill to meet us.

But below, part of the picture, now enlarged,
Confirms the impression: it seems indeed like a sea,
Except that the far shore, *l'altra sponda*, is visible here
And takes shape behind your lids, if you shut your eyes;
The visible is certainty, even when as terrible
As the hill just back then, disappearing, displaced
From lesion into lesion, and bleeding copper; but
The invisible is what constantly eludes us
Whilst whispering of its presence, persistently
Making us act, translate it into images…
Our daily labour, our laborious hope.
Next morning, after the work of the Danube
Heard all night in the hotel room, we learn the news:
Montale is dead. I have long kept
For him a single unwritten letter –
Ma è tardi, sempre più tardi
In the years which a wind is driving ever faster
Like a ship with its canvas in full bloom.
But the Danube still isn't a sea. Upstream
It's already narrower, though still raised
Above its measure, drowning ancient hearths
Where fire, with dead breath coaxing the flame,

Was wedded to the spirits of water
In a repeated act of faith. The bearded stone egg
Fixes us with a fishy stare; in its presence
We would breathe with gills if we could.
But air, inhabited by the visible, is still our certainty.
On the far shore, Trescovăț, its trapezoid
Crag of porphyry. A sign on the far shore.

Signs in the invisible, however,
We must invent – late though it may be,
Ever later. This poem, or this song,
Has to hold to that.

Five letters

   1

It was a wood along the century's ridge,
October; I remember leaves the colour of your dress,
A patch's rhombus, so carefully sewn –
As if some petty sense depended on it
That was forgotten straight away,
                                      as you spoke.
I can hear a bird singing in the egg,
There's a key in its beak
Beneath its pulsing tongue;
                                      as for the lock –
This you'll have to imagine. And the door.
Behind the door, it's summer. With our twofold shadows
Wedded on a golden ground, caught
In an unclear blessing. I love you.

The century has slipped its ring thirty-three times
Over each of those trees sewn into the sky
Like veins into a leaf, like hope
Into an indifferent certainty. I'm writing to you
From a distant province, where words are assayed
By the weight of the unsaid, and memory
By the length of its deceptive shadow. You must forgive
My handwriting: chill wraps the fist from within,
Its glove is tight, and the movement wavers
Over the dimly-sensed meaning of the sentence,
Over the initial hemmed with hoar-frost –
I forgot to tell you: it's winter here.

2

Your unwritten letters insist on a reply;
Those unread letters, memorised
In an unfuddled fever of anticipation,
In the fugue of some voyage, or in sleeplessness
Bitter and bright with your breath and the snow
On the window of this room;
       did you forget
The postcode? I breathed it, illegibly perhaps,
Into the music you love; I wrote it in the margin
Of a page in a book you're afraid to read at night,
When its truth flashes like phosphor between
The black of the print.
      My reply runs: nothing
Can dissolve the toxic glue of years
Which binds hope to space, and time to faith
In the spaces of hope.
      As for misfortune –
It's merely the sister of some absent wisdom,
The shadow, perhaps, of a foreseen defeat;

The meaning eludes me, like the meaning of music,
Which is mathematics anyway, though my calculations
Use just two or three golden numbers
Derived from your name. So, maybe,
We both end up in deficit.
      Nothing,
However, can take our place
In this pattern of effects
Penned by the numbed hand of a god
Into the amnesia of the stars, into the brief memory
Of drying ink,
Into your letters, your unwritten letters.

3

One summer you were transformed
Into your image, the one I sometimes see
In the mirror as I stand, wisely, in the shadow
Behind your shoulders: perhaps your true image,
Suddenly tangible, real, and ripe
For the bloom, like the aloe. Every move of yours
Was a restless sketch of light in air dense
And elated with August. Every touch of mine
Would leave a golden trail over your skin
Still salty to the tongue
                      with which I could only
Stammer: I love. What a summer!
(In the snapshots, the same as any other:
Fossils of light, unreliable, deceive us
When, remembering, we scrape back the strata
Of years, years, seeking a sense which has already
Shifted into some fresh expectation.)
                                  Or did I simply
Imagine all this? I think not, for evidence
Exists: the scars of a stubborn hope
Which still smarts when grazed by your voice,
Your fingerprints on the glaze of the jug
From which the wine is still evaporating
That was left undrunk in the cellar
The summer when you were transformed
Into a blessing, into your everyday miracle.

We live a time of fragmented miracles
And forgetful wisdom. Can you recall that summer?

4

Black ink clots to a coronary
In the nib of my fountain pen:
                                  so a sentence is
Broken off without warning, in an unwanted syncope.
I write it out again, but on resuming I change
The meaning first imagined.
                              The real
Meaning is now hiding in the break,
The hiatus of white, the defeat
Of a stroke just started –

If I could write you a letter of such
Breaks, such floodlit switch-rails in the track
Of sentences started in love, resuming,
Let's say, with a description of a starless sky,
If I could hold my tongue
Yet tell you all, like a leper
Standing before you with hood and rattle –

I would, perhaps, be able to tell you
Why love changes, in some unwished-for
Syncope, and on resumption is wedded
With its shadows, though it never forgets
The meaning of its name, the reasons why it lasts –

So all I can do is describe:
As if studying, committing to mind, a beloved face
By touch, like one who is blind.

5

Will you know me when we both find ourselves
Out there, in the home of our blind tenderness,
Which I once called the home of the swans?
The engraving of wrinkles round the eyes that
You will recognise, perhaps, were cut
Quite routinely, by an invisible scalpel
In some numbed hand, in time-honoured union
With the empty years. For the rest, I resemble
The double who stays in the mirror when I turn
My back, and takes aim at the nape of my neck.

But first we have so much to do:
Redeem the hostages we gave to fate
When our blood combined in the tide-race
Out to one of our possible futures,
Count the scars, stop the clockwork
Of taunts forgotten in some fevered
Regrouping, read all that lies between the lines
Of unwritten letters and memorise
Their grim cipher,
                teach bliss
To grow on stone, like moss –

Try plotting the path of lightning, to grasp
The years' unfathomed trick: time stands still
If you give it its real name. Outside the window
I can see acetylene jets tipping
The magnolia twigs. It rained last night.
I didn't tell you: here it's already spring.

Étude

Buttercup, cowslip, dandelion, chamomile –
Each tiny yellow flower reminds me of joy,
The unreasoned joy which usually goes with hope,
Like the fine embroidery on her blouse, perhaps,
If one can imagine hope in a blouse.
Translated into the tongue of music,
Tiny yellow flowers (buttercup, cowslip…)
Would ring in C major. From fields
In late spring where oil-to-be blooms
Thick, bright-yellow, in tiny flowers,
Breathing happiness into the blue. For no reason.

Between the leaves of a palimpsest
Of your years and mine, my love,
I've discovered traces of tiny yellow flowers
Between the lines describing places we love:
Hope, your little sister, was playing with our book.

Looking glass

The disc is a little husky, from long love
With the sapphire needle; each note has shifted
Into its sound-shadow, but the whole stays
Intact;
        music, too, has the power
Of adjusting insensibly, as has
The face which, already shifting into
Its next-day shadow, fixes me every morning
Through the mirror; a face already lined
By a long love with light in the air
But even more
By a long thirst for light in the blood –
Now, perhaps, Duke Ellington is chatting
With Mozart (who listens not only
Out of politeness), and so the night shifts
Into the pleasant space of a possible fate
Made to the measure of this music.

Morning Argolid

I step out onto the balcony – and below, the Argolid
In a morning hallucination as clear as crystal;
The turned lining of the cityscape thrusts me
South of the acknowledged waking world,
Sounds change sense to suit –
I hear a bird chirp: Tiryns!

I rub my eyes: the tombs of kings
Are marching down from Mycenae;
                                        masks beaten
From thin gold hang in the chestnut trees,
The poplar masses upright into a cypress,
A cat basks on a Cyclopean rampart
(Were we in Boeotia, it would grow wings) –
Then a babble of voices: the chorus is contesting
The will of the gods, but does not hinder
Its fulfilment; it stays a family matter,
The tragedy can take its course –

A sip of honey snaps me sober, a cigarette,
The morning paper, a farce in the headlines;
And yet, as I enter the bathroom
I hesitate slightly, like Agamemnon…

Acqua alta

    1

We've been together too long, Serenissima,
Down the years and the unequal quickening
Of our decays, Queen of the Sea. The spirit
Over the waters has grown weary, so why not
This eye weighed down with memory from within
(As the fruit remembers), where your images
Teem like maggots? You've gilded my retina
With the light of your air above the Lagoon,
Filled my nostrils with the sickly smells
Of canals where crumble the facades
Of musty palaces, and in the tiny bubbles
Of your glass gimcracks you've captured
The air my memories breathe. It was love and hate
At first sight: I almost still a child,
Hit in the plexus by the image, real at last,
Of the fairest of squares – whereas you
Simply behave in keeping with your nature
And experience, and press me green inside your
Insatiable herbarium, beside so many of my fellows
From the hours of vigil. Your miracle reminds me
That the meaning of myth needs re-examining
In the light of your truth, as sensed
In the chronicler's nightmares, foam cloudy
And gold on the crest of a wave roaring
In its effort to overtake the source and let
The evening and the morning be the second day.

2

Byzantium (I'm just one of the bearers
Of her spat-upon shadow) did not know she was sick
With cancer in the Lagoon, until the metastasis
Had eaten away liver, lungs, pericardium and future
In her raped insides. You smile, Serenissima,
Among the toothless winged lions, like
Our Lady among irises, in blasphemy.
These letters are black, black as the lacquer
On the gondola sliding through the orange peel
And random trash of your canals. And gold, like
The muted gold of the basilica, whose floors
Are splitting at invisible seams, to the cut
Of the years. Yet, you'll say, did I not want
Longhena to sew a temple into my heart,
Maybe just for love of a poet's love,
That schiavone's, who knew a few of love's
Secrets held otherwise under seal?
                                                              But
Your dome is collapsing into you,
Santa Maria della Salute,
The weary spirit over the waters is angry,
And its wrath roars in the irregular breath
Of the demented tide. You smile, Serenissima,
And ask: have you ever thought of death in
Venice? Over there is an island and a graveyard
Where lies another poet, who said:
What thou lovest well remains;
                                    the rest is dross.
See me as dross, but recall me
As flame, only flame.

3

Stair by stair, then into the square
(The way ambassadors of empires entered) –
Filthy water. Water from rickety foundations
Of petrified trees (Forgive me, Holy Mother…),
Water wind-lashed off the Adriatic's shallow seas
Onto the three confused inlets of the Lagoon
Poisoned in Marghera. This is how a sick century
Metes out justice and punishes the hubris of beauty,
Erected in nothingness, between two mirrors.
I see you, Queen, eaten away by pigeon-droppings
And the darkness welling from your waters' veins.
PAX TIBI MARCE EVANGELISTA MEUS,
Though your bones bob on the tide, and gold
Shivers over them, and precious stones shiver
In the gold. As four horses from Constantinople
Flare their nostrils, restive at the scent
Of the four horsemen from Patmos.

                                              Acqua alta.

I shall go first. Your decay
Quickens more slowly, Serenissima,
Look – my black dog licks my hand,
Strange benediction, in the dusk
Of an April day. We've been together too long
In the love and hate of two different transiences.
And may the spirit over the waters have mercy upon us,
In all its absence, may it have mercy.

FROM
Script

Pismo

1992

In praise of sleeplessness

Unsleeping eyes which do not only see
The patterns on the wall and morning's stain
Can read a future summer's history
That's written out in longhand by the rain –
For each leaf's destiny there is a line
Which maps its form: each drop's semantics dream
The future garden's shape, or the design
Of empty skies which scintillate and scream.

The dreadful blessing of a waking night
Is felt when patience unbraids, from inside,
The eyes, and widens out the roots of sight
To build new roads where new-seen shapes can ride –
A star is bursting into blooms of sea,
And in a glass of water, silence glitters,
Time after time your pasts keep breaking free,
And oceans taste so beautiful, so bitter.

Insomnia brings a fresh sleep into play:
Your waking self works on another plane –
Made in yesterday's image, the new day
Has grown a shadow, and is not in vain;
Your acts – you take your coat, your key ignites
The engine – are precise but other-led;
Polysemy sings at the traffic lights,
And weaves new cloth with triple-coloured thread…

All those who feel at night that time's unsure
Will give a different structure to their day,
From hour to hour; bound by its simple law,
They ask: Is there a structure anyway?

Insomnia spawns another sort of sleep:
The waking state which recreates you teems
With this new form of sleep, as waters seep
Through desert sands. And in it, freedom gleams –

The sleepless know of different nights: those where
A star is bursting into blooms of sea,
Primeval forests, choking, drink the air
And water of a summer still to be;
Last image: sleepless eyes, just like a rear-
View mirror filled with road as it's unrolled
Into the void, glimpse Eden as they peer
Into the final sleeplessness, the fold.

Octaves on summer

If a shadow hardens right at summer's start
And twines its way, like a vein in marble, through
This June, you know the summer will burst apart
Prematurely from inside, and split in two
Round Elijah's Day; twin powers with one heart
Still hold your once-taut threads; but they're releasing
Them now, impassively, and the speed's increasing
As, all the while, the fall is wearying you.

Wind in the drained glass on the balcony slows
By early evening, settling to dregs of grit.
A butterfly in your heart. You feel you chose
To surrender your fall-back line, pawning it
For an absent mercy. On the road which flows
To the skyline, the gleam of distance is just
Starting to hem the dark, and the cloud of dust
Behind the rider who is bearing the writ.

The flutter of purple rags at dawn! All this
Is moving pictures – gardens tumbling downhill,
And towers plunging up into the abyss,
The upturned chalice overhead! It's a thrill
Which you've dressed up in words, like the imprecise
Future scried by a prophet who doesn't know
How, when let loose, imagination can grow,
Like contaminated wine, a haze of vice!

This will ripen into summer, perfecting
It when the Fates impassively ordain,
When future time and past, in their connecting
Vessels, both settle into a single plane.

Meanwhile the heart still keeps the herald in sight,
His winged heels, gauging their distance and speed –
And hears the cries of the passing cranes recede
Into mists of darkness on their rain-soaked flight.

from **Strambotti**

1

I can feel the silence glistening in
The semi-darkness while you breathe at night,
And hear the pulse beneath your temple's skin
Beside me, on the pillow to my right;
But when the sun draws close, your sleep grows thin,
Though mine won't touch my eyelids till first light:
For years we've slept in syncopated time,
And all the while our love matures like wine.

2

I lie awake beside you till the day
Rips, with its nails, the hem of sky behind
The boughs. I know what shapes your dreams replay –
Nightmares, remembered gardens – through your mind,
And read your nightly journeys in this way
On a beloved face that's still unlined:
Till dawn distils your travels to a bare
Print on the pillow, and the scent of hair.

3

When I ask what you dreamt last night, you say
You do not know, or smile; so might it be
That you forget your dreaming straight away,
Or you don't want to solve the mystery?
Perhaps it was a wasteland, cold and grey,
And hence forgetting is your remedy:
Instead of poems I wish that I could write
Legible abstracts of your dreams each night!

4

*For years I've known that we are disappearing
Together*, I wrote when time formed the brow
Of a wave with youth's salty foam still searing
Across it, white-hot, bright with passion; now
I'm all the surer that we'll end up shearing
Away together: two late fruit whose bough
Is shaken, as the day draws to an end,
By a gardener's steadfast, gentle hand.

5

Can you feel this acceleration, bringing
Spaces together, letting them accrete
In us like honey in the comb? This thinning
Of distances like foil: beyond, a fleet
Of unknown stars, a darkness, the beginning
Of the unnoticed, and a fierce black heat –
But this side of the thinned-out foil, there's room
For a late spring. One where magnolias bloom.

8

The world we see and its own double lie
Outlined in the glittering of your aura;
I am a cell-bound monk, a butterfly
Cocooned, in the world outside you. And for our
World's equation we're binomials, y
And x. That's not how Petrarch spoke to Laura;
The pattern is the same, though. And the thread.
Conversing soul to soul, Socrates said.

9

We are twin foci of the same ellipse,
The orbit of a body that's unknown –
A star? Or light which thinks of weight, perhaps,
Along its journey's gyre out there alone?
We are twin foci of the same ellipse
Who're bound together at the distance shown
To match the line precisely, hand-in-glove,
Which links two other foci: death and love.

10

As you breathe on the pillow to my right,
I listen to the zodiac's slow arc
Above the flat roof, voices in the night
Which colours in the space between the sparks
Of stars; the world comes closest when we're quite
Alone, when its soul whispers from the dark
To teach us wisdom: that of spending time
With silence, while our love matures like wine.

Never lonelier

Never lonelier than in late July,
With summer's zenith just a foot away,
But chlorophyll a cubit from decay,
From metastasing into gold and brown,

When colours shade towards a darker green
In gardens, while in fields the stubble's dry;
And darker, lower amplitudes now chime
In winds that blow all through the night, through time.

Never lonelier than in late July,
When you think all is in your grasp: each sense
Is keener, like a knife still blue with heat

From the grindstone, although the core's not there.
You sense an angel whom you'll never meet,
Yet benediction fills the pregnant air.

Pietà

> A Mother's heart is the Madonna's heart
> TIN UJEVIĆ

I slid both of my slender hands beneath
Your shoulders, lifting them a little way –
A slow act which reminds me of the move
I used to make when changing you; I raised
You lightly from your horizontal balance,
As if you were not heavier by a death
(Your sacrifice's weight was taken from
The scales). Since then you've lain forever in
My arms, beyond illusion and the real;
The world's restored here, through this move of mine
And through the love behind your deed, outside
Me, and it's brought back on an even keel.

I slid both of my slender hands beneath
Your shoulders, lifting them a little way;
And turned to stone now, this is how we'll stay.

Sea
Jeremiah, 31. 3

An oil-leak from the primum mobile,
For aeons now the sea's been losing heat
But keeps on running to the inner beat
Of its first cause; the blue beneath the spray
Teems with the larvae of the world that we
Perceive, and the suspicion now unfurling
That it might shape-shift to a beast, to whirling
Molecules and fire: the roar of the sea.

Although that sum can't be reduced to mere
Amounts, it's parsed to scenes inside your mind,
Which balks at thoughts of endlessness with bounds:
The sea lasts on as shards, as glints, in sound's
Faint after-images which stay behind
When storms have passed, and freeze inside the ear
As quietness; you cannot hope to know
The secret, real name of that blue, and so

You say: the sea, at which your thoughts veer round
At random – ships, a quay, a summer day –
Since, by routine, imagination plays
The sixth sense back as images and sound.
You'd like eternity to fit your need
To put it into words, and so you feed
The flame in which all mortals burn away,
Forever as the self-same paraphrase

Of some forgotten master copy. Sea,
Sea seen in sun, and booming through some stranded
Columbus's recurring nightmare, or

Meek waters which comply with the decree
That heaven's sluice-gates should stop off the flood.
Sea, lackey to the power which commanded
That it be, sea of muscle and of blood,
Blood from the ur-beast that's its metaphor –

An hour-glass which unceasingly revolves
So no abyss is ever drained; sea glimmering
With sweat, in beauty tempered with the chill
Of horror, its best match; as sea dissolves
The flesh, so sea dissolves the evening star,
The angels' tongue is crushed to flowers and tar
In its dark maelstrom, its black cauldron simmering
To serve its God with steadfast, dreadful skill.

Whatever you might plunge into the sea
Is lighter by the weight of pain displaced,
As Archimedes showed; the bronchial tree
Of one who's drowning shatters in the forced
Baptism – this transfiguration's blessed,
Though, by the nature of the will which caused
Its pain, for all things living are at best
A curve of imperfection: life is graced.

Don't blame the sea. And do not even blame
The emptiness which hides in the unsaid.
It all falls back to one pure line, look, ruled
By the horizon when the seas turn tame
And grow like fingernails of those who're dead,
In motionlessness; everything is spooled
Back to a quiet whose normality
Echoes a whisper in Gethsemane.

Perhaps the primum mobile has rusted
Fast, after the creation of the aim
Which proved its Maker right; the world's not going
To give up on the effort of foreknowing
Its shifts of shape. To keep faith, all the same,
With this foreknowing is the loyalty
Of sailors who, right till the end, have trusted
The sea.
       That roaring, listen: it's the sea.

FROM
Four Canons

Četiri kanona

1996

from **First canon**

    3

The Lord kills and makes alive, goes about
His work in our daily lives, like a gardener:
He grafts, he weeds, he prunes, and he burns
Damp heaps of leaves in late autumn; smoke
Pricks our eyes, tears sting more bitterly still.

He goes about his work like a nurse: bustling without
A word, he adjusts a pillow, threads a needle into a vein,
His are the fingerprints on the bottle dispensing mercy
Drop by drop; he changes a dressing stained with blood
Like the wine-stained tablecloth after the last supper.

He brings down to the grave and brings up; besides,
Enterprises are established by him: your nail can't crush
A flea against your thumbnail if it's not forewritten.
He weaves the gale into the night, pounds the ship to pieces,
And dyes the wool black on a mother's distaff.

The Lord dismembers and reassembles things
Which can be said and felt: he shatters, rends and joins,
Solders, glues and welds, he sutures without stitches
As it suits him: the waves of the sea, for instance.
And those who stumbled are girded with strength by him.

Ocean star, you who are a walled garden, can you see
This rift at the heart of things we love? Can you hear
The diseased murmur in the beating heart of the world?
Meanwhile the millennium gutters like a host of candles
Before an empty tomb, in Jerusalem.

4

Lord, I have heard your speech, and was afraid –
It was tongue-tied but terrible, as if dug out of the
Quivering guts of Kopaonik, that hulking mountain
Where the spruce loom tall, and Jerusalem sage blooms yellow.

In wrath remember mercy, I thought in my heart –
But what if you're asleep, and your eyes
Are beyond all wrath? Perhaps you're just twisting
And groaning in some ugly, discordant dream.

Things turned ugly on the eighth day of creation.
You cleaved the earth with rivers, mud flows along their beds.
Perhaps you really are asleep – fatelessly, in the words
Of the poet, that harmless prisoner in the tower by the Neckar.

The mountains saw you, and they trembled; so why not
A heart which cannot see you, but still reveals
Your mark, as an ECG reveals a scar:
Speaking it in love, in revolt, in doubt –

Cold is the earthly milk I drink each morning;
And you who are his Milkgiver, check on him
While he's sleeping, scrape the sweat from his eyebrows…
And pray for me: may he forgive my fear
That he created me, as the book says, in his own image.

from **Second canon**

2

Here in the dark night of the soul, rebuke
Dries out the scab upon a wound not cleansed
By any village healer's blade, nor bathed
With mercy-giving herbs. And sleeplessness
Burns underneath the scab, on such a night;
Vengeance is yours, and recompense, it's said.

Why aren't you leading me about, why don't
You make me to suck honey from the rock,
And oil out of the flinty rock, or eat
The produce of the fields upon the heights
Of earth? And Jacob, your fine paradigm,
Is mired in scandal in the soul's dark night.

But Jacob is the rope that measures your
Inheritance: it dangles in the eighth
Day's empty hut, throughout the soul's dark night,
This howling wilderness; from emptiness
Your stage designer builds a sacrilegious
Set, for vengeance is yours, and recompense.

On such a night, there's not the slightest swish
Of an archangel's wing, uparching like
A parachute to float your mercy down
Into this place of horror, howling wilderness:
On such a night, recrimination reigns,
And all the stems of hope are choked with weeds.

On such a night, you douse the signal fire,
That star which flickers just above the sea,

Which radiates a sacred light and sends
A beam of mercy's photons through the gloom –
Yet by this star you calculate your course,
Yes, even when you hide your face in darkness.

    5

It is written that your dead shall live,
As if they weren't already here, mingling with the shadows
In air that's pitted with our voices,
Those taciturn assistants in the effort of recall
Crucial for stepping briskly back from the void,
Those mute off-stage prompts when we stumble over forgotten lines

Crucial for when we have to come up with an answer
To an unasked question; they're everywhere, except perhaps
In cemeteries, where the unthinking seek them, in love
With their own error; where frozen-fingered lighters of grave-lamps,
Priestesses of rotted leaves and protectresses of blown-out candles
Go about their business, sisters to the flapping of ravens

Above the age-old lime trees.
                                      What's more, it is written
That you will establish peace for us, for you have done
All our works for us. Which also means that you breached
A ceasefire this morning with an incident in the no-man's-land
Between two hatreds, hidden by the smokescreen of fog
Above your sick River Danube. But your dead shall live,

Those who dwell in dust shall awake and sing –
And between the hazardous shadows of your visible deeds
They place an invisible arm round our shoulders: unpredictable
Allies, strangers and family, holograms projected

At odd moments into a colourful dream, just before dawn.
Your dead shall live, together with my dead body they shall arise,

And you who are clothed with the sun, with the moon under your feet,
Pray for the dead, pray for the unborn, pray for the souls
Intermingled with things past and to come, both of which
Will weigh us down the same when placed on the pan
Of a dispassionate set of scales.
                                    And mention my soul as well,
In a motherly, gentle conversation.

Translator's notes

Fresco (34)
In a letter to me, Lalić wrote that this poem is 'A combination of two frescoes: one is the famous white angel from Mileševa [Monastery], and the other exists only in my mind'.

Byzantium (36)
The medieval Byzantine Empire had a huge cultural, religious and political influence on the emerging Slav states to the north and west. In 1204, Venice, its trading rival, persuaded the Fourth Crusade's leaders to sack the Byzantine capital Constantinople (formerly called Byzantium). Fatally weakened, the Empire could not resist the later advance of the Ottoman Turks, who conquered the Balkans from the 1380s onwards. They finally took Constantinople in 1453, killing the last emperor Constantine XI (who had asked the Pope for military help, but to no avail).

Death with a falcon (38)
Despots were local rulers allied to (or vassals of) the Byzantine and Ottoman Empires: the title had no connotation of tyranny. According to his biographer, Serbian Despot Stefan Lazarević died in 1427, apparently of a stroke while hunting.

Melissa (39)
Lalić wrote that Melissa was 'a righteous woman who lived on the Isthmus. Demeter initiated her into her mysteries, about which she was sworn to secrecy. When the other women could not coax the secret out of her, they tore her to pieces. As punishment, Demeter sent a plague to that region, but changed Melissa's remains into a swarm of bees.'

The Argonauts (42)
'the stars / Where we clumsily wrote our names': *Argo Navis* (the Ship Argo) became a constellation. Robert Graves' *The Greek Myths*, which Lalić owned, links the Argonauts' voyage with the signs of the zodiac. Jason, the Argo's captain, old and an outcast, tried to hang himself from its prow, but it collapsed and killed him.

Marina (44)
In T.S. Eliot's 'Marina', Pericles travels the seas, seeking his daughter Marina. Lalić admired Eliot's work, and he and Branka Lalić translated Eliot's poem for their 1972 *Anthology of Modern American Poetry*. In Serbian, *Marina* also means 'Seascape'.

Three squalls of rain (45)
The bora is a strong wind from the mountains that can blow up in the Adriatic, especially between late autumn and early spring. It can also bring rain.

Atlantis (48)
The epigraph is abridged from Plato's *Timaeus*.

Algol (61)
In 1978, hearing I was interested in astrology, Lalić gave me a book from his father's collection: Fehlow's *Course in Scientific Natal Astrology* [*Lehrkursus der wissenschaftlichen Geburtsastrologie*], published in Thüringen, Germany in 1934. About the star Algol, in the constellation of Perseus, it says (in my translation):

> From the Arabic *al-ghoul*, the demon. A dark companion circles the main star once every 69 hours, cutting off its light for 9 hours at a time. The ancient Chinese observed the change in light and said: full brightness means there will be dead as the sands of the sea, especially when Mars is near […]. The Babylonians called it 'the Boomerang' – or, as we would say nowadays, the guillotine of the heavens, for near the Sun it gives the risk of beheading. A famous example: Robespierre, who caused the violent death of many, only to end up on the scaffold himself […] It must be pointed out, however, that the star also has higher spiritual influences, to which only the most highly-endowed individuals are receptive. This may be the case with Mussolini.

Mussolini's own violent end, in 1945, would have been unwise to predict in Nazi Germany. Lalić said that the theme of this cycle was the fear of nuclear annihilation.

Winter morning (66)
Serbian poet Vojislav Ilić (1860–94) was an important influence upon Lalić's poetry. Pelagonia is a lowland district of the then-Yugoslav *republika* of Macedonia – a good 100–150 kilometres from the Aegean. Xenophon's *Anabasis* ('Ascent') recounts how 10,000 Greek mercenaries became stranded deep in Persian territory after an abortive coup, and had to make for the safety of the Greek cities on the Black Sea.

Spring liturgy for a dead poet (68)
The works of Serbian *poète maudit* Branko Miljković (1934–61) are obsessed with death as the final, incommunicable experience, where the poem is the sole survivor. He was found hanged from a tree in a Zagreb park one February morning, aged 27.

Aosta (74)
An Alpine valley in northern Italy.

Nereid (79)
Of this poem, Lalić wrote: 'Even today I enjoy that game in which a cove (on Red Island, near Rovinj) changes into a woman, and back again'.

Tomb in Prague (83)
The tomb of Rabbi Judah Loew ben Bezalel (*c.* 1525–1609) stands in Prague's Old Jewish Cemetery. A revered Talmudic scholar, astronomer, mathematician, and kabbalist philosopher, he became the focus of legends. One was that of the golem, a being he was said to have created from clay to protect the Jewish community.

Skopje's monologue (85)
Skopje was devastated by an earthquake early in the morning of 26th July 1963. Over a thousand people were killed, and hundreds of thousands left homeless. After a huge national and international relief effort, the city was rebuilt.

Orange (91)
The Croatian poet Dobriša Cesarić (1902–80) also wrote a poem called 'Orange'.

Joanna from Ravenna (94)
In the mosaic of Byzantine Empress Theodora and her court in Ravenna's Basilica of San Vitale, Joanna stands two places to the Empress's left. The daughter of the commander Belisarius, she was renowned for her beauty.

The masons (96)
Dubrovnik was shattered by an earthquake in 1667.

Portal: pietà (97)
The Pietà, dating from 1498, stands above the doorway to the Franciscan Church – the only part of the Franciscan Monastery to survive the 1667 earthquake.

The Dark Province (98)
A Balkan folktale tells how a king was riding through the Dark Province. He heard a voice say: *If you stop to pick us up, you'll regret it; if you pass us by, you'll regret it.* He looked round, but could only see pebbles, so he put one in his pocket. When he regained the world of the living, it had turned into a diamond.

*** (103)
'But still I think…': the quotation is from Sappho.

Belgrade from Old Photographs (113)
Quotations are from *At the Kalemegdan*, by early 20th-century Serbian poet Milan Rakić. The 'Clock Tower' is on the Kalemegdan fortress, which lies above the city. Vračar, in Rakić's time, was a new suburb. 'The Scales' (Terazije) is a square that forms Belgrade's official centre-point. Nearby is Republika Square, with the equestrian statue of 19th-century Serbian Knez (Prince) Mihailo Obrenović. 'Dreadnought Tower' (Nebojša kula) is an octagonal medieval tower on the Kalemegdan.

Cantico delle creature (117)
Lalić wrote to me: 'Since this poem came into being, I've been back to Assisi. St Francis's tomb is now air-conditioned. And so this poem becomes a sort of document of cultural history'.

Letter to John Berryman on hearing of his death (118)
John Berryman: American poet and academic (1914–72).

Daphne (120)
Mount Athos, the monks' republic in northern Greece, is the spiritual centre of the Orthodox faith. Access, for men only, is by boat to the port of Daphne; thereafter, travel is only possible on foot. 'Close to joy and hard to grasp' plays on the opening of Hölderlin's poem 'Patmos': 'Close / And hard to grasp is the God.'

Byzantium VIII, or Chilandari (122)
Chilandari monastery was founded by Serbian King Stefan I Nemanja in 1198. His son, Archbishop Sava, Serbia's patron saint, is also buried there. The 'miracle': a story tells how St John of Damascus, falsely accused of treachery, had his hand severed in punishment. After praying all night to an icon of the Madonna, which now hangs in Chilandari, his hand was miraculously joined back to his arm.

Mnemosyne (124)
Mnemosyne was the Greek goddess of memory, mother of the Muses. Aquileia was a Roman port, now 2 km inland from the Venetian lagoon; its basilica has a fine 4th-century-CE mosaic floor. Attila's tent turned blood-red three days before his murder. '*In the wind, the weathervanes are rattling*': the ending of Hölderlin's poem 'Half of Life [Hälfte des Lebens]'. 'Heraclea' is Heraclea Lyncestis, an ancient Greek city near

Bitola, North Macedonia; it has the remains of early Christian basilicas with mosaic floors.

The spaces of hope (132)
From Kanfanar Station in Istria, a branch line led to Rovinj, Lalić's second home.

The raven's monologue (133)
After the rain stopped, Noah sent out a raven from the ark: it 'went forth to and fro, until the waters were dried up from off the earth' (Genesis 8). Then he sent a dove.

Elegy, or the Danube at Donji Milanovac (134)
At the Iron Gates gorge between Serbia and Romania, the Danube was dammed for a hydroelectric project, and the Serbian town of Donji Milanovac moved uphill to the banks of the resulting lake. Mount Miroč features in a folk epic about mythic hero Kraljević Marko and a *vila* ('wood-witch'), a female spirit akin to the Greek naiad. Upstream lay the 8000-year-old village of Lepenski Vir; the crag of Trescovăț across the river was probably sacred to its inhabitants, who left pebbles carved into fishlike human figures or heads (some bearded). '*Ma è tardi, sempre più tardi* [*But it is late, ever later*]' is from Eugenio Montale's 'Dora Markus' (1939). The last lines of Lalić's poem echo those of Hölderlin's 'Patmos': 'so that the solid / Letter, and what exists, be well / Interpreted. German song holds to that.'

Five Letters: 5 (136)
'Which I once called the home of the swans' – an early poem by Lalić, 'The home of the swans', begins:

> You see, I know that out there, in the home
> Of blind tenderness, the lost paradise of the unspoken,
> The swans are living […]

Morning Argolid (143)
The Argolid, in the Peloponnese, is far to the south of Lalić's Belgrade apartment.

Acqua alta (144)
Acqua alta ('high water') is the tidal peak that regularly floods Venice. Longhena was the architect of Santa Maria della Salute, opposite the Riva degli Schiavoni (Shore of the Slavs). This poem's *schiavone* is Laza Kostić;

'Your dome is collapsing into you, / Santa Maria della Salute' pastiches his 1909 poem about the church. Venice is built on wooden piles; for these and her ships, much of Dalmatia was stripped of forests. Kostić asks the Virgin to 'Forgive me, mother of the world, forgive me' for having thought ill of this, as they also supported her church. The 'other poet' is Ezra Pound. Marghera is an industrial town on the mainland. The horses on St Mark's Basilica were looted from Constantinople when the city was sacked, at Venice's instigation, in 1204.

Octaves on summer (151)
The Orthodox feast-day of the Prophet Elijah falls on the 2nd of August.

Strambotti (153)
The *strambotto* is an Italian poem-form, often addressing the beloved. Poem 4: '*For years I've known that we are disappearing / Together*': from 'Love' (47).

Never lonelier (156)
Lalić's poem echoes Gottfried Benn's poem of the same name: 'Einsamer nie' (1936).

Sea (158)
'heaven's sluice-gates': Genesis 7. 11.

First canon: 3 (162)
After I Samuel 12. 1-10.

First canon: 4 (163)
After Habakkuk 3. 2-19. Kopaonik is Serbia's largest mountain range. Hölderlin's poem 'Hyperion's Song of Destiny' (*'Hyperions Schicksalslied'*) has the lines 'Fatelessly, like the sleeping / Baby, breathe the celestial ones'. Hölderlin, a schizophrenic, spent the second half of his life in a tower room overlooking the Neckar. 'Milkgiver': on icons, the Madonna nursing.

Second canon: 2 (164)
After Deuteronomy 32. 1-43. Occasionally, Lalić uses a wording from the Serbian Bible which has no English counterpart – as here, where the Serbian has 'Jacob is the rope of your inheritance' (32. 9) and English-language Bibles use words like *lot*. Then I follow the Serbian – though here I was inspired by the Jubilee Bible's *measuring line*.

Second canon: 5 (165)
After Isaiah 26. 9-20. Mount Avala lies south-east of Belgrade. 'A woman clothed with the sun, with the moon under her feet' is the 'great sign' in Revelation 12. 1.

ABOUT THE TRANSLATOR

Francis R. Jones was born in Yorkshire in 1955. He studied languages, literature and linguistics at the universities of Cambridge, Sarajevo, Reading and Newcastle. He is Emeritus Professor of Translation Studies at Newcastle University, and lives in Northumberland. Jones translates poetry, mainly from Bosnian-Croatian-Serbian and Dutch into English. He has also worked from Russian, Hungarian and Caribbean languages, and into Yorkshire and Geordie dialect.

Jones has published 16 solo-translated collections. These include seven volumes by Ivan V. Lalić, and one by Dutch poet Esther Jansma, *What It Is: Selected Poems* (Bloodaxe Books, 2008), with another translation from Dutch, *About Time: Selected Poems* by Gerrit Kouwenaar forthcoming from Bloodaxe. His English version of Bosnian poet Mak Dizdar's *Stone Sleeper* (Anvil Press Poetry, 2009), has been translated onward into six other languages. His translations have also appeared in chapbooks and jointly-translated volumes, in journals and anthologies.

Jones's translations have won no fewer than 15 prizes. These include the prestigious European Poetry Translation Prize twice, for his versions of Ivan V. Lalić. And his translation oeuvre from Dutch gained him the 2005 inaugural James Brockway Prize for the Translation of Dutch Poetry.

EU DECLARATION OF GPSR CONFORMITY

Books published by Bloodaxe Books are identified by the EAN/ISBN printed above our address on the copyright page and manufactured by the printer whose address is noted below. This declaration of conformity is issued under the sole responsibility of the publisher, the object of declaration being each individual book produced in conformity with the relevant EU harmonisation legislation with no known hazards or warnings, and is made on behalf of Bloodaxe Books Ltd on 20 November 2025 by Neil Astley, Managing Director, editor@bloodaxebooks.com.

No part of this book may be used or reproduced in any manner for the purpose of training artificial intelligence technologies or systems. The publisher expressly reserves *The Taste of Lightning* from the text and data mining exception in accordance with European Parliament Directive (EU) 2019/790.